AN
OBSERVATION
SURVEY

OF EARLY LITERACY
ACHIEVEMENT

MARIE M. CLAY

AN

OBSERVATION

SURVEY

OF EARLY LITERACY ACHIEVEMENT

HEINEMANN

Published by Heinemann Education, a division of Reed Publishing (NZ) Ltd, 39 Rawene Road, Birkenhead, Auckland, New Zealand. Associated companies, branches and representatives throughout the world.

In the United States: Heinemann, a division of Reed Publishing (USA) Inc. 361 Hanover Street, Portsmouth, NH 03801-3912

ISBN 0 86863 288 0 (NZ)
ISBN 435 11004 7 (UK)

© 1993, Marie M. Clay
First published 1993
Reprinted 1993, 1994 (three times), 1995 (with updates) (twice), 1996 (four times), 1997 three times

Library of Congress Cataloging-in-Publication Data

Clay, Marie M.
   An observation survey: of early literacy achievement/Marie M.
Clay.
      p.   cm.
   Includes bibliographical references and index.
   ISBN 0-435-08763-0
   1. Reading (Primary) — New Zealand. 2. Reading (Primary) — New Zealand — Ability testing. 3. English language — Composition and exercises — Study and teaching (Primary) — New Zealand. 4. English language — Composition and exercises — New Zealand — Ability testing. 5. Observation (Educational method) I. Title.
LB1525.C56 1993   92–46100
372. 4'049 — dc20   CIP

Printed in Hong Kong

The pronouns she and he have often been used in this text to refer to the teacher and the child respectively. Despite a possible charge of sexist bias it makes for clearer, easier reading if such references are consistent.

The author and publishers permit the following observation record sheets to be copied by teachers for use with children. The commercial use of any of these observation record sheets is strictly prohibited.

- Running Record Sheet
- Record of Book Level
- Letter Identification Administration Sheet
- Letter Identification Score Sheet
- Concepts About Print Score Sheet
- Word Test Administration Sheet
- Word Test Score Sheet
- Writing Vocabulary Observation Sheet
- Writing Vocabulary Weekly Record Sheet
- Hearing and Recording Sounds in Words (Dictation Task) Observation Sheet
- Observation Survey Summary Sheet
- Observation Summary for Multiple Testings

CONTENTS

THE OBSERVATION SURVEY: PART TWO

5   Other Observation Tasks   43

6   Summarising the Observation Survey Results   71

7 The Teacher and the Observations 80

Appendices

References and Further Reading 90

Index 92

INTRODUCTION

I have been a teacher of young children, a teacher in special education, a school psychologist, and a teacher of school psychologists. I have also carried out research in developmental psychology, and in that role I have observed how children change over time as they learn more and more from all their environments — both children who make good progress and children who find it hard to learn.

My work has produced some systematic observation measures which are used widely in New Zealand and in other countries and which have been reported in the research literature. With these measures teachers observe:

- Oral language, and a child's control over sentence structures and inflections
- The reading of continuous text (running records)
- Letter knowledge
- Reading vocabulary (words known in reading)
- Writing vocabulary (words known in writing)
- Concepts about print (how print encodes information)
- Hearing sounds in words (dictation)
- Making links between those sounds and letters.

There are many other kinds of systematic observation, like the retelling of stories (McKenzie, 1989; Morrow, 1989), and approaches to more advanced story writing but I have limited the account in this book to the observation tasks which arose out of my own research.

So this book describes some observation tasks which have been used by New Zealand teachers for the last 20 years to guide their teaching of young children in formal school programmes (Department of Education, 1985). I will discuss how these observations can be made, and why we need to make them in the first years of school.

FOR WHOM IS THIS BOOK WRITTEN?

This book is for classroom teachers who want to be careful observers of young children learning to read and write. It will help teachers who work with any kind of beginning literacy programme to monitor the progress of their children, but for those who like to watch children in an open, relatively unsequenced programme of learning to read and write, observation procedures like these are essential.

This book is also for teachers who work individually with children having temporary difficulties with literacy learning. It is for administrators who want teachers to give them easy-to-read accounts of individual progress made by children between two points of time. It is for students of emerging literacy behaviours who are training themselves to be observers of learners. And it is for researchers probing how young children learn about literacy because the observation tasks have proved themselves to have sound measurement qualities.

To use systematic observation the teacher has to set time aside from teaching to become a neutral observer. One assumes that training will accompany any attempts to use the observation tasks. A teacher who tries to make them work from the written account in this book is unlikely to find as much value in them as a teacher who is able to discuss what comes from the observations with colleagues, for in such discussion the reader can test his or her understanding of the text against the (possible) meanings intended by the author.

A RICHER ACCOUNT OF WHAT IS OCCURRING

The observation procedures reported in this book arose out of a theory of how young children learn to manage the complex task of reading continuous text, described in greater detail in another book (Clay, 1991).

Despite my training in measurement and my experience in clinical child psychology I have come to regard normative, standardised tests as having a place in education, but as indirect ways of informing teachers about learning. By comparison with the observation of learners at work, test scores are mere approximations or estimates, at times misrepresenting individual progress in learning, and at times presenting results stripped of the very information that is required for designing or evaluating sound instruction. They need to be supplemented at the classroom level with standardised or systematic observations of children who are in the act of responding to instruction, observations that are reliable enough to compare one child with another, or one child on two different occasions.

The child works on his own theories of how things work in language learning and changes those theories in the face of conflicting evidence. What I like about observation is that I can watch the child at work, see something of the focus of his attention, watch him search for cues and for confirmation. I can watch him solve a problem, sometimes showing his delight in a new discovery.

Therefore, for the first two years of schooling, and especially for programmes where children are encouraged to become readers and writers of texts which are not part of a sequenced curriculum, observation records are more useful than the estimates of tests or the intuitions of informal/casual observations. The observations needed are the result of a closer look than the teacher normally has the time to take. They inform the teaching process, the parents and the administrators. They can feed data into the analyses of researchers, and best of all, they provide evidence of learning on repeated measurements of tasks the child is actually undertaking in the classroom. *In every way the information that is gathered in systematic observation reduces our uncertainties and improves our instruction.*

1 OBSERVING CHANGE IN EARLY LITERACY BEHAVIOURS

AN INTRODUCTION TO SYSTEMATIC OBSERVATION

Observation in classrooms

Observation of what goes on in classrooms has uncovered differences in time allocations which suggest that high progress children get more opportunities to learn than low progress children. Studies have produced evidence of how the successful children tend to get better and better, drawing away from the average or below-average children whose progress proceeds at an apparently slower rate. However, this slow rate of learning can occur because children do not get the kinds of help they need to learn at faster rates.

Observing individual progress

If we attend to individual children as they work, and if we focus on the progressions in learning that occur over time, such observations can provide feedback to our instruction. Observations which lead us to modify our instruction are particularly appropriate in the formative stages of new learning, as in beginning reading, beginning writing and beginning mathematics.

I have tried to observe individual children at work, reading and writing, and to capture evidence of the progress that they make. Science is based on systematic observation of phenomena under known conditions. Physicists or chemists in laboratories, botanists and zoologists in the field, and behavioural scientists in psychology, sociology, linguistics and cultural anthropology all use observation to get research data. Despite some lingering mistrust of observation in educational research, it is becoming more acceptable to use direct observation as a method for data collection, particularly in the years of early childhood education (Genishi, 1982).

With good reason educators have relied on systematic testing rather than systematic observation of learning. The measurement theories that are used to guide test construction and research analyses lead to better interpretations of test and examination results. But as we have improved our testing strategies we have placed undue emphasis on testing to the point where we can deprive teachers and administrators of valuable information about learners and their learning. There is a seductive efficiency about final assessment scores. Yet a funny thing happens on the way to those final assessments: day-to-day learning takes place. In education, we need to pay more attention to the evaluation of learners who are on the way to those final assessments. One of the things that a class teacher needs to know is what occurs over time for the individual learner in a particular classroom programme.

We do need research endeavour which looks for explanations of what causes what, or what conditions bring about differences, and such questions call for the use of a variety of research paradigms, but for effective instruction we also need answers to two basic questions: 'What typically occurs for children like those I teach as learning takes place over the school year?' and 'How is this individual child changing over time in relation to what typically occurs?' Teachers who have answers to these questions will be more responsive to the daily learning of their pupils and will deliver more appropriate feedback.

In developmental psychology young children were always studied by direct observation. Studies of how children learn to speak have been exciting, and so have the more recent studies of young children learning to read and write. But teachers must go beyond reactions like 'Ooh! Ah!', or 'I am surprised!' and 'Isn't that cute!' and try to understand what is happening and why it is happening.

Measuring outcomes

Historically, most assessment has been directed to the outcomes of instruction. We wait until the end of the instruction sequence before we assess. We

- monitor for national performance
- assess the effectiveness of schools
- assess the effectiveness of teachers
- assess primary school outcome achievements
- assess secondary school outcome achievements.

When we measure the outcomes of teaching with important tests the instruction of the learners is already over. The test score is, in legal terms, after the fact. It is almost too late to change the fate of the students because of what we find out. The opportunity has gone.

We do not have to test all children to assess educational standards at the national, state, or district level; we can use sampling methods to get information on standards in the same way that we take public opinion polls. We do not need to test every child to know whether the school system is producing satisfactory outcomes. And in many countries there is some agreement that this measurement of the education system can be done best from the age of nine years and upwards.

Measures of outcome tell us where the achievement levels of the education system lie. They do not tell us what brought about those achievement levels. We do not know from the assessments how the high achievement levels were obtained, or why the low achievement levels occurred. If we try to use those results to improve instruction

- we can only guess how to change our teaching
- we can only guess how to change our policies
- we can only guess what factors produced the scores.

Measuring abilities

Measurement theory has allowed us to measure the abilities of individual learners — intelligence, language skills, auditory and visual perception, and so on. When we measure these things we *predict* how well an individual student might learn in our programmes. This type of testing is usually done before instruction and it has resulted in children being grouped according to estimated abilities.

Even when we give these tests to individuals we score them according to what we know happens to groups of children. We predict for individuals from *group* data, not from individual data. We use norms, or average scores for children of the same age. Such predictions are often wrong for individual children.

If teachers do use outcome tests and ability scores, and many will be required to do so, they should be aware that every expectation they hold of what a child can and cannot learn should be mistrusted, in the sense of holding a tentative hypothesis that can be revised. For if we give the learner particular opportunities and the right learning conditions, that learner might prove the test's predictions to be wrong. Teachers should always leave room to be surprised by individual children.

Every test score has some error of measurement attached to it; there is error in group scores, and error in individual scores. We should keep an open mind on what is possible for the individual child to achieve. We have in the past sometimes made assumptions about children that closed the possibility of their learning more.

When our predictions are wrong for individual children, education practices tend to deprive those children of opportunities to learn. We keep them away from certain challenges (we keep them out of school, or we hold them back to repeat the same class with the same curriculum, or we give them less to learn, or we give them drastically simplified tasks).

Assessments that guide our teaching

Effective teaching calls for a third kind of assessment designed to record how the child works on tasks and to inform teaching as it occurs. To use the metaphor of a football game, you do not improve the play of a team by looking at the outcome score. The coach must look closely at how the team is playing the game and help them to change the moves or strategies that produce a better final score.

When the class teacher observes how individual children are problem-solving, it makes a difference to what happens in classrooms. It is particularly useful in three kinds of situations:

- for young children up to eight years of age
- at the introduction of new areas of learning
- when the activity being learned is complex.

Classroom teachers can observe students as they construct responses by moving among them while they work. They can observe how individuals change over time by keeping good records. And they can allow children to take different learning paths to the same outcomes because they are clearly aware of the learning that is occurring.

Such teachers are like craftsmen, monitoring how their products take shape. Think of the painter or potter adjusting the light, shade, colour, shape or texture of a product in formation. Or we could think of the violinist in the orchestra who knows that one of his strings is slipping off pitch. He takes an opportunity during a pause in the performance to avert disaster by tightening the string. He would not wait for the critic's review of the performance in the morning paper, saying one violin was out of tune! Skilled craftspeople fine-tune the on-going construction or performance. Teachers should work in this way.

To improve teaching teachers need to observe children's responses during literacy instruction

- for competencies and confusions
- for strengths and weaknesses
- for the processes and strategies used
- for evidence of what the child already understands.

Observing oral language

Early childhood education has used observations of what children can do because little children often cannot put into words what they are doing or thinking.

In the past 25 years, studies of how children learn to speak have been exciting. In the 1960s researchers went into homes to observe children learning language and record its use as it occurred in natural settings. They followed the progress of particular children as they developed and their language changed. They studied what actually occurred, making precise records, and they did not depend on tests or on recollections of what occurred (Brown, 1973; Paley, 1981; Wells, 1986).

Interest shifted from an early focus on the structures of language to meaning. In the 1970s this led us to study the effects of the contexts in which language occurs. The young child's language is so related to the things he is talking about that you can have trouble understanding him unless you also know about the things he refers to. We became more sensitive to the ways in which we change our language according to the place we are in, and who we are talking to. We learned more about the ways in which the languages of the homes differ, more about dialects and more about the complexities of bilingual learning.

Attention moved to the detailed study of interactions between mothers and children, teachers and children, children and children. As a result of all this recording of naturally occurring behaviour we now know a great deal about the ways in which the contexts of language inter-

actions facilitate or constrain the development of language in children. We know that entry into formal education settings such as schools reduces children's opportunities for talking, and that some types of programmes prevent children from using the excellent and efficient ways of learning language which they used before they came to school (Cazden, 1988).

Observing emerging literacy

There have been many exciting observational studies of children's writing since the 1970s. The young child has emerged as an active participant in the process of becoming a writer. To take only one illustration, the studies of Mexican and Argentinian children by Ferreiro and Teberosky (1982) described the fascinating shifts occurring well before children begin to use the alphabetical principle of letter-sound relationships, which we commonly think of as the beginning of writing. These preschool children were making discoveries about writing, constructing the writing system and making it their own. The observation of early writing behaviours has taken us forward in great leaps since 1975.

Many observers discovered that preschool children explore the detail of print in their environment, on signs, cereal packets and television advertisements. They develop concepts about books, newspapers and messages, and what it is to read these. Case studies over long periods of time show how children change over time and how more advanced concepts emerge out of earlier understandings.

Preschool children already know something about the world of print from their environments. This leads them to form primitive hypotheses about letters, words or messages both printed and handwritten. It is a widely held view that learning to read and write in school will be easier for the child with rich preschool literacy experiences than it is for the child who has had few opportunities for such learning.

We have learned of these things mainly through research which has used observation rather than experimentation as its method. When we become neutral observers and watch children at work in systematic and repeatable ways we begin to uncover some of our own assumptions and notice how wrong these can sometimes be.

Observing school entrants

Systematic observation of school entrants has distinct advantages over readiness testing. At entry to school children have been learning for five to six years, since they were born. They are all ready to learn more than they already know. Why do schools and educators find this so difficult to understand? Teachers must find out what children already know, and take them from where they are to somewhere else.

When we give a 'readiness test' to a new school entrant we are trying to predict school progress from what a child already knows (see Measuring abilities, page 4). We are merely asking 'Are you ready for my programme?' Readiness tests divide children into a competent group ready to learn on a particular programme and a problem group supposedly not ready to learn. On the other hand, observations which record what learners already know about emerging literacy eliminate the problem group. *They are all ready to learn something*, but are starting from different places.

Suppose we observe the literacy behaviours of a group of new school entrants. Some know a little about reading and writing and others know very little. Those who know very little may have paid almost no attention to print in their preschool years because they had little opportunity or encouragement, or no incentive or interest. Or perhaps some adults around them tried to teach them and the children found the tasks very confusing and so withdrew their effort to learn. Undoubtedly, what the young child knows about literacy when he or she enters school is not a matter of competency unfolding from within, for in an oral culture where literacy does not exist, no such behaviour unfolds. It is a matter of opportunities to learn about a very arbitrary symbol system. There will be individual differences for other reasons but the one aspect of this development that we can influence and foster is in the area of appropriate opportunities to learn. That usually means providing a responsive environment within which the child can explore and negotiate meanings.

When children enter school we need to observe what they know and can do, and build on that foundation whether it is rich or meagre.

The New Zealand teachers I worked with in various research projects did observe children when they entered school and taught to expand the various competencies that children already had. They taught in ways that introduced children to print in reading and in writing activities so that they could learn more than they already knew. They gave more help and more attention to the children who knew the least, making up for missed opportunities to learn.

The observation tasks used in this Survey are *not*

readiness tests which sort children into who is ready to face literacy learning and who is not. In particular the Concepts About Print (CAP) task is not a readiness test because it only samples one dimension of a child's preparation for formal instruction. However, '...in the United States...the CAP tests have tended to be used in kindergarten in much the same way that readiness tests are often used' (Stallman and Pearson, 1990). While those authors look to the construction of better commercially available tests of readiness, I strongly support the abandonment of the readiness concept in its old form. All children are ready to learn; it is the teachers who need to know how to create appropriate instruction for where each child is. To do this effectively they need to observe a wide range of literacy behaviours throughout the first years of school. (See also Clay, 1991, page 19.)

My theoretical analysis of beginning reading and writing tells me that children have to extend their knowledge along each of several different dimensions of learning as they approach formal literacy instruction. At the same time they have to learn how to relate learning in any one of these areas (say letter learning) to learning in any other (say messages and meanings). Along each of these dimensions more learning has to occur. It does not happen in an orderly way. It is not the same for all children. Each learner starts with what he or she already knows and uses that to support what has to be learnt next.

To become observers of the early stages of literacy learning teachers will have to give up looking for a single, short assessment test for the acquisition stages of reading and writing. Children move into reading by different tracks and early assessments must be wide-ranging. If there is a single task that stands up better than any other it is the running record of text reading. This is a neutral observation task, capable of use in any system of reading, and recording progress on whatever gradient of text difficulty has been adopted by the education system. (See pages 20 – 42; also Johnston, 1992.)

Standardised tests do not measure slow progress well

It is difficult to design a good reading assessment instrument which can be used close to the onset of instruction. Standardised tests sample from all behaviours and they do not discriminate well until considerable progress has been made by many of the children (Clay, 1991, page 204). Yet teachers can identify the children making slow progress before standardised tests can do this effectively. In my own research 20 to 25 percent of beginning readers were showing some confusions and difficulties one year to 18 months before good assessments could be obtained by standardised tests of reading for children in the tail end of the distribution of test scores. We should try to use systematic observation by teachers as one way to achieve early identification of children who need supplementary help.

I have come to place less emphasis on assessments which yield an age or grade level score in the first years of school. A programme of assessment will give me checkpoints on the general level of performance of children but I would want to have, in addition, records of progress on individual children — where they were at various points during the year, what products they could produce and what processes they could control on what texts.

To be acceptable as evidence of children's progress observational data would have to be as reliable as test data. Running records have shown high reliability, with scores for accuracy and error having reliabilities of 0.90. Observers find self-correction behaviour harder to agree upon and the reliability can drop to 0.70.

Running records of text reading have face and content validity. You cannot get closer to the valid measure of oral reading than to be able to say the child can read the book you want him to be reading at this or that level with this or that kind of processing behaviour. Little or nothing is inferred. You can count the number of correct words to get an accuracy score. The record does not give a measure of comprehension but you can tell from the child's responses to the story and from the analysis of error and self-correction behaviour how well the child works for meaning. And you can gauge his understanding of the story in the discussion you have with him about the story. You do not get a score on letters known, but you can see whether the child uses letter knowledge on the run in his reading.

In summary, standardised tests are indirect ways of observing children's progress. They are suitable for reporting the behaviours of groups but cannot compare with the observation of learners at work for providing the information needed to design sound instruction.

Systematic observation

Educators have done a great deal of systematic testing and relatively little systematic observation of learning. One could argue that educators need to give most of their attention to the systematic observation of learners

who are on the way to those final scores on tests.

Systematic observations have four characteristics in common with good measurement instruments. They provide:

- a standard task
- a standard way of setting up the task (administration)
- ways of knowing when we can rely on our observations and make reliable comparisons
- a task that is like a real world task as a guarantee that the observations will relate to what the child is likely to do in the real world (for this establishes the validity of the observation).

The standard task and administration provide sound measurement conditions. Otherwise we would be evaluating with a piece of elastic instead of using an instrument that behaves in the same way on every occasion. Two measurements with a piece of elastic cannot be compared; and comparability is often important not only at the national, state and district level but also at the individual level. For we often want to compare a student on two of his own performances. A standard task, which is administered and scored in a standard way, gives one kind of guarantee of reliability in comparisons.

Not all of our observations have to be on standard tasks but those used to demonstrate change over time should be. The problem with observations is that they can have many sources of error. One of these sources of 'error' is that what you 'know' about reading and writing will determine what you observe in children's literacy development. You bring to the observation what you already believe.

We need to design procedures that limit the possibilities of being in error or being misled by our observations. One way we can do this is to make certain that a wide range of measures or observations is used. Probably no one technique is reliable on its own. When important decisions are to be made we should increase the range of observations we make in order to decrease the risk that we will make errors in our interpretations.

For example, a word test should never be used in isolation because it assesses only one aspect of early reading behaviours. So does retelling. The child is learning more about letters, and about how print is written down, and how to form letters and write words, and something about letter-sound relationships, and teachers need to know how learning is proceeding in each of these areas. That is why the observation tasks described in this Survey range across each of these areas of knowledge.

It is imperative, also, that we attend to the reliability of our observations. An unreliable test score means that if you took other measures, at around the same time or at another time, you might get very different results. We have to be concerned with whether our assessments are reliable because we do not want to alter our teaching, or decide on a child's placement, on the basis of a flawed judgement. We need to be able to rely on the data from which we make our judgements.

It is important that we use tasks that are authentic. The word authentic has arisen among educators because many tests of reading and writing and spelling are being challenged as not valid measures of real world literacy activities. One of the current criticisms of the multiple choice type of test items is that they are a special type of task not found in real life; they are a test device with no real world reference. It will be better if we can find sound assessment procedures which reflect what the learner is mastering or struggling with. (Concepts About Print was designed to have such authenticity 20 years before the word appeared in the assessment field.)

Characteristics of observation tasks

All the observation tasks which I will discuss were developed in research studies. I like to call them observation tasks but they do have the qualities of sound assessment instruments with reliabilities and validities and discrimination indices established in research studies.

These observation tasks can be justified not only by theories of measurement: other theories are taken into account, from the psychology of learning, from developmental psychology, from studies of individual differ-

ences, and from theories about social factors and the influences of contexts on learning.

The observation tasks were *not* designed to produce samples of work which go into portfolios; they were designed to make a teacher attend to how children work at learning in the classroom. It is useful to supplement our observations of children's portfolio work by systematic observation tasks, because portfolio products are often channelled by the teacher's ways of teaching or expectations, and sometimes a different kind of observation task will confront the teacher with a new kind of evidence of a child's strengths or problems.

The observation tasks in this Survey do not simplify the learning challenge. They are designed to allow children to work with the complexities of written language.

They do not measure children's general abilities, and they do not look for the outcomes of a particular programme. They tell teachers something about how the learner searches for information in printed texts and how that learner works with that information.*

---

*To help teachers attend to features of oral language one could recommend Clay et al. (1983) and Cazden (1988). A standard story retelling task (McKenzie, 1986; Morrow, 1989) is also helpful to sensitise teachers to individual differences in the child's growing control over constructing stories.

2 | READING AND WRITING: PROCESSING THE INFORMATION IN PRINT

THE READING PROCESS

Reading, like thinking, is a complex process. The reader has to produce responses to the words the author wrote. In some way the reader has to match his thinking to the author's.

You will be familiar with the old game 'Twenty Questions' or 'Animal, Vegetable or Mineral'. Reading is something like that game. The smarter readers ask themselves the most effective questions for reducing uncertainty; the poorer readers try lots of trivial questions and waste their opportunities to reduce their uncertainty. They do not put the information-seeking processes into effective sequences.

Many instructional programmes direct their students to the trivial questions. All readers, from five-year-old beginners on their first books to the effective adult reader need to use:

- their knowledge of how the world works
- the possible meanings of the text
- the sentence structure
- the importance of order of ideas, or words, or of letters
- the size of words or letters
- special features of sound, shape, and layout
- and special knowledge from past literary experiences,

before they resort to left to right sounding out of chunks or letter clusters or, in the last resort, single letters. Such an analysis suggests that the terms 'look and say' or 'sight words' or 'phonics' are grossly simplified explanations of what we need to know or do in order to be able to read.

Reading for meaning involves the reader in working with information from all these resources. Even after only one year of instruction, the high progress reader operates on print in an integrated way in search of meaning, and reads with high accuracy and high self-correction rates. He reads with attention focused on meaning. What he thinks the text will say can be checked by looking for sound-to-letter associations. He also has several ways of functioning according to the type of reading material (genre) or the difficulty level of the material. Where he cannot grasp the meaning with higher level strategies he can engage a lower gear and use another strategy drawing on knowledge of letter clusters or letter-sound associations, but all the while the competent reader manages to maintain a focus on the messages of the text.

On the other hand, the low progress reader or reader at risk tends to operate on a narrow range of strategies. He may rely on what he can invent from his memory for the language of the text but pay no attention at all to visual details. He may disregard obvious discrepancies between his response and the words on the page. He may be looking so hard for words he knows and guessing words from first letters that he forgets what the message is about. Unbalanced ways of operating on print can become habituated when they are practised day after day. They become very resistant to change. This can begin to happen in the first year of formal instruction.

That is why systematic observation of what the child can do and where his new learning takes him is so important in the first year of school. Close and individual attention from a teacher at this stage can help children to operate on print in more appropriate ways, so they can learn to work effectively under normal classroom conditions and make progress at average rates.

In recent years there have been shifts in our understanding of some psychological processes and yet old theories remain encapsulated in our teaching methods and assumptions. Some of these concepts need to be reviewed here.

[handwritten margin note: need to comprehend what is being read]

By far the most important challenge for the teacher of reading is to change the ways in which the child operates on print to get the messages. We must look briefly at the model of the reading process that is implied here. (A more extensive discussion related to the early years of formal schooling is available in Clay, 1991.)

1 Reading involves messages expressed in language. Usually it is a special kind of language which is found in books. Children bring to the reading situation a control of oral language but the oral language dialect differs in important ways from the written language dialect. Although some children may not speak the same oral dialect as the teacher almost all have a well-developed language system and they communicate well in their homes and communities. They have control of most of the sounds of the language, a large vocabulary of words which are labels for quite complex sets of meanings, and they have flexible ways of constructing sentences.

*dialect in reading & speaking differs

2 Reading also involves knowing about the conventions used to print language — direction rules, space formats, and punctuation signals for new sentences, new speakers, surprise or emphasis, and questions. These are things which the skilled reader does not think about because he responds giving only minimal attention to such conventions of print. But for the beginning reader they are the source of some fundamental confusions.

*Grammar not paid attention to x. Too confusing

3 Reading involves visual patterns — clusters of words/syllables/blends/letters — depending on how one wants to break the patterns up. Processing information from the printed page is so fast in skilled readers that it is only by drastically altering the reading situation in experiments that we can show how adults scan text to pick up cues from patterns and clusters of these components. Young children tend to operate on visual patterns in very personal ways and slowly enough for us to observe some of what they do.

Processing info.

4 The flow of oral language does not always make the breaks between words clear and young children have some difficulty breaking messages up into words. They have even greater difficulty breaking up a word into its sequence of sounds and hearing the sounds in sequence. This is not strange. Some of us have the same problem with the note sequences in a complicated melody.

breaking message in wds.

These are four different areas of learning which facilitate reading. Language was discussed first because the meanings embodied in print are of high utility, especially if one already knows something about the topic of the text. Language has two powerful bases for prediction in reading. The first is the meanings and the second is the sentence structures. A third, less reliable and sometimes confusing and distorting source of cues exists in the letter-sound relationships. Theoretical analyses tell us that it is the consistencies in the spelling patterns or clusters of letters, rather than the letter-sound relationships, that assist the mature reader's reading. If that is where the consistencies lie that is where the human brain will find and use them.

The conventions that printers use to print language also need to be learned because we need to attend to the visual information in ways that follow the rules of the printer's code, more or less.

Visual information is essential for fluent correct responding and skilled readers tend to use visual knowledge in a highly efficient way, scanning for enough detail to check on the messages of the text. The beginning reader must discover for himself how to do this scanning and how to visually analyse print to locate cues and features that distinguish between letters and words.

The sound sequences in words (which linguists call the sequence of phonemes) are also used in rapid reading to anticipate a word from a few cues or to check a word one is uncertain about. This requires two kinds of detailed analysis in strict coordination; the analysis of the sounds in sequence and the visual analysis in left to right sequence.

Most children can become literate. They can learn literacy behaviours if the conditions for learning are right for them as individual learners. Three shifts in knowledge about learning have raised our expectations for greater success for more children in literacy learning today. Firstly, it is accepted today that experience counts in cognitive functioning, and some of what we thought of as 'given' in intelligence is learned during the process of cognitive development. Secondly, there has been a shift away from the belief that 'in some rough and ready way' achievement matches to general measured intelligence. We have known for nearly 30 years that when you look at the children who are over-achieving, for example when a child is reading well and several years above his mental age level, then the supposed match between achievement and intelligence must be questioned.

If we put the last two concepts together — that some part of the cognitive process is learned or realised through experience and that achievement ages do not necessarily match mental ages — there is plenty of scope for teaching and learning experience to bring about a change in children's attainments.

The third revision of an older position is in the area of brain functioning. When psychologists wrote about the brain as similar to a telephone exchange, association theories of learning were popular and people were thought of as having better or poorer telephone exchanges, prewired to do poorer or better jobs. Without discarding the idea that people may differ in the brain structures they have to work with, it is now known that for complex functions the brain probably constructs circuits which link several quite different parts of the brain and that such circuits only become functional for those persons who learn to do those things. We create many of the necessary links in the brain as we learn to engage in literate activities. If we do not engage in literate activities we do not create those linked pathways.

THE WRITING PROCESS

The exploration of literacy that preschool children do is even more obvious in their early attempts to write. They explore the making of marks on paper, from scribble to letter-like forms, to some letter shapes, often part of their own name, to favourite letters and particular words and then they acquire more letters and more words, but all the time invented forms and invented words intrude into their productions as they explore possibilities. After entry to school children work quite hard to understand the conventions of the printer's code, the 'rules' of writing language down, mastering some of these quite early, and taking a surprisingly long time to understand the functions of others, for example, the space concept, or the importance of order, or the difference that orientation of letters makes to what they stand for.

For example, Amanda's writing looks like a jumble of disoriented letters but the teacher who observed her rated it a good attempt at the observation task which records how well the child can hear the sounds in words.

In fact preschool children can respond to and learn about visual features of print, know some letters, write some words, make up pretend writing as letters to people, or dictate stories they want written, and all this before they have begun to consider how the words they say may be coded into print, and in particular how the sounds of speech are coded in print. The biggest hurdle is to learn when this coding follows regular rules or patterns, and what are the alternate or irregular coding patterns that might be needed.

Without a feel for the conventions of print the child cannot bring what he knows about letters and words to bear on the writing task, and without some skill at hearing the sounds within words, he has no chance of learning letter-sound relationships. He may memorise some letter sequences of words he likes to write using

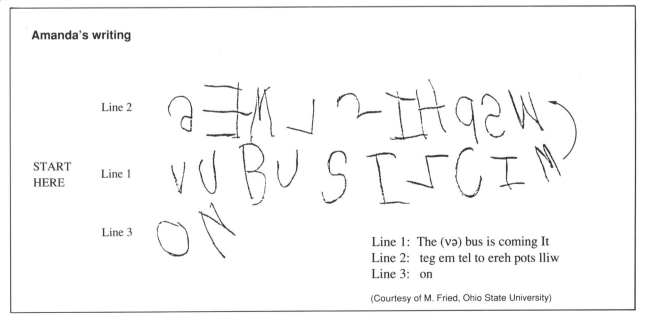

Amanda's writing

START HERE — Line 1, Line 2, Line 3

Line 1: The (və) bus is coming It
Line 2: teg em tel to ereh pots lliw
Line 3: on

(Courtesy of M. Fried, Ohio State University)

visual information and a memory for the motor movements. But until he begins to notice that sounds in his speech can be written in consistent ways he has no way of attempting to write a word which he has not memorised.

So, there are many facets to the writing process just as there are to the reading process, and they can be described in much the same way. Writing involves messages expressed in language, and the writer must compose these. They flow directly from his own language competencies. Writing involves visual learning of letter features and letter forms, and patterns of letters in clusters or in words, and mingling these with what one knows about the conventions of the printer's code. Writing also involves the young writer in listening to his own speech to find out which sounds he needs to write, and then finding the letters with which to record those sounds.

As the young writer works earnestly to get his message down on paper he is, like the reader, working up and down the various levels at which we can analyse language — message, sentence, word, letter cluster, or letter-sound. As a reader he may ignore some of the information in print, leaning upon the anchor points of the information he knows. In writing, however, there is no other way to write than letter by letter, one after the other; it is an analytical activity which takes words apart. He may omit letters, or use substitutes for the ones

in orthodox spelling, but he is forced by the nature of the task to act analytically on print when he is writing.

Composing orally something that he wants to write, or wants a teacher to write for him, is not easy for all children and the quality of composition, in telling stories or relaying information, improves as children immerse themselves in the task (Paley, 1981).

There is, however, a tedious time when the child must work out for himself how the composition can be recorded, and what he, as the writer, has to do to get the story down on paper. Both the composition and the scribing sides of the task can be approached with success by the preschool child, or in the first year of school.

In summary, teachers aim to produce independent readers whose reading and writing improve whenever they read and write. In the independent student:

* early strategies are secure and habituated
* the child *monitors* his own reading or writing
* he *searches* for cues in word sequences, in meaning, in letter sequences
* he *discovers* new things for himself
* he *cross-checks* one source of cues with another
* he *repeats* as if to *confirm* his reading or writing
* he *self-corrects*, assuming the initiative for making cues match, or getting words right
* he *solves* new words by these means.

3 ASSISTING YOUNG CHILDREN MAKING SLOW PROGRESS

TRADITIONAL APPROACHES

Since I first began to teach children to read more than 40 years ago the teaching problems have remained much the same, although the services have increased and improved and the percentage of children needing special help may have been reduced. What we do have today is an awareness of literacy learning among teachers, parents and the community that did not exist in the 1950s when we were trying to create that awareness.

With the growth of community interest there has been a proliferation of naive ideas about what reading is and what reading difficulties are. Incorrect and misleading ideas are found in the media each week. The following are two examples.

- Critics of the schools often assume that people differ in intelligence but they expect all people to reach a _similar_ level in reading. These two expectations are contradictory.
- Completely erroneous statements are made about words _seen in reverse_ or _the brain scrambling the signals for the eyes_ or _squares looking like triangles._ There is no evidence to support such nonsensical descriptions of how our brains work as we read.

These errors of understanding arise from adults who make superficial or poor observations of their own skills or who disseminate misguided interpretations of new concepts, half-understood.

By the fourth year of school a teacher will have a range of reading ability in her classroom that spreads over five or six years. The less able children will read like children in the first or second year class and her more able children will read like young high school pupils. There is a range of reading achievement for which the class teacher must provide. It comes about in part because once a certain command of reading is attained one's reading improves every time one reads.

Traditionally _a child has been considered worthy of special help only if his achievement falls more than two years below the average for his class or age group. That criterion had more to do with the reliability of our achievement test instruments than with any particular learning needs of the children._

Teachers and the educational system should make every effort to reduce the number of children falling below their class level in reading, but public opinion must learn to ask appropriate evaluative questions. If all children at every point in the range of normal variation are increasing their skill then the school is doing its job well. All children will not be able to read in the same way or at the same level any more than they can all think alike.

Let me give an example. Livia had many differences in his preschool experiences compared with the average school entrant. He was over seven years before he was able to start reading books. In his fourth year at school he was reading well at the level of children in their third year at school. In one sense he was not a reading problem. His rate of progress _once he had begun to read_ was about average. Livia needed reading material and instruction _at his level_ so that he could continue to learn to read and only in that sense had he a reading problem. If given harder materials to read he would work at frustration level and could even 'go backwards' because he would no longer be practising, in smooth combination, the skills he had developed so far. In this way he could become illiterate for want of appropriate pacing of his reading material.

There is a reading level below which the child may lose his skill when he moves out into the community rather than maintain it. It falls somewhere around the average 10- to 11-year-old reading achievement level. If our reading skill is not sufficient for us to practise it every day by reading the paper or notices or instructions, then we seem to lose some of the skill in much the same way as we lose a foreign language which we no longer speak.

A first requirement of a good reading programme is that all teachers check the provisions that they make for the lowest reading groups in their classes. Is the programme really catering for the range of literacy knowledge which the children have? For learning to occur it is *very* important to ensure that the difficulty level of the reading material presents (challenges) from which the child can learn, and (not difficulties) that disorganise what he already knows. If children in a low reading group are not reading for meaning, if what they read does not sound like meaningful language, if they are stuttering over sounds or words with no basis for prediction, they should be taken back to a level of reading material where they can orchestrate all the reading processes and knowledge into a smoothly functioning, message-getting process. (They will read fairly accurately with about one error in five to 10 words.)

give challenging material not difficult [handwritten margin note]

Each classroom needs a wide range of reading books to cater for the expected range of reading skills. All children need both easy and challenging books from which they learn different things. Just as you might find it relaxing on holiday to pick up a light novel, an Agatha Christie or a science fiction book, competent readers enjoy easy reading too. *On easy material they practise the skills they have and build up fluency.*

Perhaps one or two children in the lowest group do not seem to be able to read anything. It may be that they have been forced to read at frustration level for as long as a year or two, and they may even have *lost their initial reading skills.* Children can go backwards later in their schooling, reading worse than they did at an earlier age. Such children may need individual teaching in order to redevelop an independent attack on books.

In the lowest reading group of many classes there could be a child who has never started to learn to read. Such children may be given remedial attention two and three times a week for several years yet they do not catch up to their peers; they may gain some reading skills but do not usually make up for those years of lost learning and their associated sense of failure.

What are the ingredients of a good reading programme for children of low achievement in classroom settings? For a good programme you need a very experienced teacher who has been trained to think incisively about the reading process and who is sensitive to individual differences. You need an organisation of time and place that permits such teachers to work individually with the children who have the least skills. The teacher

helps and supports the pupil in reading meaningful messages in texts which are expertly sequenced to the individual's needs.

The teacher aims to produce in the pupil a set of behaviours which will ensure a self-extending system. With a self-extending set of behaviours the more the learner reads or writes the better he gets, and the more unnecessary the teacher becomes.

The teacher expects to end up with pupils who are as widely distributed in reading as they are in the population in intelligence, mathematical achievement, sporting skills or cooking prowess. But each pupil should be making progress *from where he is to somewhere else.*

Frequently, someone approaches me with this kind of statement: 'I'm not a teacher, but I would like to help children with reading difficulties. Do you think I could?' My answer is that the best person to help a child with reading difficulties is a trained teacher who has become a master teacher of reading, and who has been trained as a specialist in reading problems. There is no room for an amateur approach to children with reading difficulties, for, unlike many human conditions, failure to read almost never ends in spontaneous recovery.

EARLY INTERVENTION

All understandings of how we read and of what the reading process is have changed in the last two decades under the impact of reports from intensive research efforts. What the older scholars recommended as techniques still have validity (for example, Fernald, 1943); the ways in which they understood the reading process do not. Theorists now look upon the reading process in a different way and that makes many of the older texts on reading out of date. It is not enough today to recommend old concepts and cures to solve reading difficulties. We now have very good reasons for discarding old concepts that lead to ineffective teaching.

If I believed for example that visual images of words had to be implanted by repetition in children's minds, and that a child had to know every set of letter-sound relationships that occur in English words before he could progress in reading then I could not explain some of my successes as a teacher. I could not explain how an 11-year-old with a reading age of eight years could make three years' progress in reading in six months, having two short lessons each week. It just would not be possible. A good theory ought at least to be able to explain its successes.

When I surveyed research reports which measured children before remedial work, after the programmes, and then after a follow-up period, the results were almost always the same. Progress was made while the teacher taught, but little progress occurred back in the classroom once the clinical programme finished (Aman and Singh, 1983). One study like this carried out in New Zealand recently had the same result. The children could not continue to progress without the remedial teacher. They were not learning reading the way that successful readers learn. *Successful readers learn a system of behaviours which continues to accumulate skills merely because it operates.* (Exceptional reading clinicians do help children to build self-extending strategies but they do not seem to do this frequently enough to influence the research findings.)

We have operated in the past on a concept of remedial tuition that worked but did not work well enough. There have been clinicians, principals, teachers, and willing folk in the community working earnestly and with commitment. Individual children have received help but the size of the problem has not been reduced. Some children were recovered, others were maintained with some improvement and some continued to fail.

Why was this so? Lack of early identification has been one reason. In other areas of special education we practise early identification. Deaf babies, our blind and cerebral-palsied preschoolers and others with special handicaps get special help to minimise the consequential aspects of their handicaps. Yet a child with reading difficulties has had to wait until the third or fourth year of school before being offered special instruction. By then the child's reading level is two years behind that of his peers. The learning difficulties of the child might be more easily overcome if he had practised error behaviour less often, if he had less to unlearn and relearn, and if he still had reasonable confidence in his own ability. Schools must change their organisation to solve these problems early. It takes a child with the most supportive teacher only three to four months at school to define himself as 'no good at that' when the timetable comes around to reading or writing activities.

Teachers and parents of 11- to 16-year-olds often believe that schools have done nothing for the reading difficulties of the young people they are concerned about. Yet the older child has probably been the focus of a whole sequence of well-intentioned efforts to help, each of which has done little for the child. This does not mean that children do not sometimes succeed with a brilliant teacher, a fantastic teacher-child relationship, a hard-working parent-child team. What it does mean is that the efforts often fail *for want of experienced teaching, and for want of persistence and continuity of efforts. They often fail because they are begun too late.*

It seemed to me that the longer we left the child failing the harder the problem became and three years was too long. The results of waiting are these.

- There is a great gap or deficit to be made up.
- There are consequential deficits in other aspects of education.
- There are consequences for the child's personality and confidence.
- An even greater problem is that the child has not only failed to learn in his three years at school, he has tried to do his work, he has practised his primitive skills and he has habituated, daily, the wrong responses. He has learned; and all that learning stands like a block wall between the remedial teacher and the responses that she is trying to get established.

A remedial programme must take what has to be unlearned into account.

Why have we tended to wait until the child was eight or more years old before offering special assistance?

- We believed, erroneously, that children mature into reading.
- We do not like to pressure children, and we gave them time to settle.
- We knew children who were 'late bloomers' (or we thought we did).
- Our tests were not reliable until our programmes were well under way and we were loath to label children wrongly or to use scarce remedial resources on children who would recover spontaneously.
- We did not understand the reading process sufficiently well.
- We thought a change of method, a search for the great solution, would one day make the reading problem disappear.
- We believed in simple, single causes such as 'not having learned his phonics'.
- Teachers have real difficulty in observing which children are having difficulty at the end of the first year of instruction, often claiming there are no such children in their schools.

In 1962 when I began my research I asked the simple question 'Can we see the reading process going wrong in the first year of instruction?' It was, in terms of our techniques at the time, an absurd question. The answer is, however, that today this can be observed by the well-trained teacher. And it is much simpler than administering batteries of psychological tests or trying to interpret the implications for reading of neurological examinations.

At the end of the first year at school, teachers can locate children who can be seen to need extra resources and extra help to unlearn unwanted behaviours or to put together isolated behaviours into a workable system. Simple observation tasks will predict well which young children who have been in instruction for one year are readers 'at risk'. The children's performance on the tasks also gives the teacher some idea of what to teach next. The second year at school can then be used as a time to catch up with the average group of children.

THE SENSITIVE OBSERVATION OF READING BEHAVIOUR

First steps in the prevention of reading difficulties can be taken in any school system by the sensitive appraisal of the individuality of school entrants, and the careful observation at frequent intervals of children's responsiveness to a good school programme. Predictive tests may be available but are prone to error because they try to estimate how well a child will perform in an activity he has not even tried yet. They can be supplemented or replaced by systematic observation and recording of what children are doing as they perform the tasks of the classroom. Observation of children's behaviour is a sound basis for the early evaluation of reading progress. Children may stray off into poor procedures at many points during the first year of instruction.

I refer here to a controlled form of observation which requires systematic, objective recording of exactly what a child does on a particular (sometimes contrived) task. It must be carried out without any accompanying teaching or teacher guidance. This contrasts with several things — observation while teaching, casual or subjective observation, or judgemental conclusions based on remembered events from fleeting observations during the teaching of many children.

Of 100 children studied in one Auckland-based study (Clay, 1966; 1982) there were children making slow progress because of poor language development and whose real problem lay in their inability to form and repeat phrases and sentences. There were many children who wavered for months trying to establish a consistent

directional approach to print. There were children who could not hear the separation of words within a spoken sentence, nor the sequence of sounds that occur in words. Some children attended only to the final sounds in words. Two left-handed writers had some persisting problems with direction, but so did several right-handed children. For some children with poor motor coordination the matching of words and spaces with speech was a very difficult task. But other children with fast speech and mature language could not achieve success either, because they could not slow down their speech to their hand speed. They needed help with coordinating their visual perception of print and their fast speech. There were unhappy children who were reticent about speaking or writing, and there were rebellious and baulky children. There were children of low intelligence who made slow progress with enthusiasm, and there were others with high intelligence who worked diligently and yet were seldom accurate. There were those who lost heart when promoted because they felt they were not able to cope, and others who lost heart because they were kept behind in a lower reading group.

A flexible programme which respects individuality at first, brings children gradually to the point where group instruction can be provided for those with common learning needs.

While sensitive observation during the first year of instruction is the responsibility of the class teachers, a survey of reading progress after one year of instruction should be programmed by a person responsible for organisation and evaluation of the first years in school. Such a survey is held to be desirable and practical, in addition to the observations made by class teachers.

A year at school will have given all children a chance to settle, to begin to engage with the literacy programme, to try several different approaches, to be forming good or bad habits. It is not hurrying children unduly to take stock of their style of progress a year after society introduces them to formal instruction. Indeed, special programmes must then be made available for those children who have been unable to learn from the standard teaching practices. This makes good psychological and administrative sense.

The timing of such a systematic survey will depend upon the policies of the education system regarding:

• entry to school
• promotion and/or retention.

In New Zealand continuous entry on children's fifth birthdays is usually followed by fixed annual promotion to the third-year class level. This allows a flexible time allocation of 18 to 36 months for a child to complete the first two class levels according to an individual child's needs. A slow child who takes a year to settle into the strange environment of school may need extra help in the second year to make average progress before promotion to class or year three.

A different scenario would occur with fixed age of entry. Children entering school at one time (four-and-a-half to five-and-a-half, or five-and-a-half to six-and-a-half) would be surveyed within or after their first year at school. My preference would be for them to receive individual help at the beginning of the second year, having been promoted rather than retained. An alternative would be to get help to them after six months of the first year on the assumption that they could be promoted to the second-year class rather than retained. This latter procedure may lead to some unforeseen problems in that it may identify for help children who would 'take off' without help in the second six months of that first year of school.

In school systems where entry occurs at younger ages more relaxed and less urgent policies can be adopted. In systems where entry age levels tend to be higher, formal instruction tends to proceed with more urgency and waiting for a year before identifying children may not be seen as appropriate. The key point to bear in mind is that children must not be left practising inappropriate procedures for too long, but on the other hand they cannot be pressured and hurried into learning the fundamental complexities of reading and writing. This leads us back to the child who is having difficulty with school learning towards the end of his first year at school.

Each child having difficulty will have different things he can and cannot do. Each will differ from others in what is confusing, what gaps there are in knowledge, in ways of operating on print. The failing child might respond to an intervention programme especially tailored to his needs in one-to-one instruction.

THE EARLY DETECTION OF READING DIFFICULTIES

Traditionally reading difficulties have been assessed with readiness tests, intelligence tests, and tests of related skills such as language abilities or visual discrimination. These have been used to predict areas which might account for a child's reading failure. The problem with the intricate profiles that such tests produce is that while they may sketch some strengths and weaknesses in the child's behaviour repertoire, they do not provide much guidance as to what the teacher should try to teach the child *about reading*. The child with limited language skills must still be taught to read, although some authorities advise teachers to wait until the child can speak well. The child with visual perception difficulties can be put on a programme of drawing shapes and finding paths through mazes and puzzles, but he must still be taught to read.

Many research studies have found no benefit resulting from training programmes derived directly from such test results. The pictorial and geometrical stimuli used with young retarded readers did not produce gains in reading skill. And oral language training was no more useful. This may well be because the children were learning to analyse data which they did not require in the reading task and they were not learning anything that was directly applicable in the reading activity. Again and again research points to the egocentric, rigid and inflexible viewpoint of the younger, slower or retarded reader. And yet statements on remediation just as often recommend training the child on 'simpler' materials — pictures, shapes, letters, sounds — all of which require a large amount of skill to transfer to the total situation of reading a message which is expressed in sentence form! To try to train children to read on pictures and shapes or even on puzzles, seems a devious route to reading. One would not deny that many children need a wide range of supplementary activities to compensate for barren preschool lives; but it is foolish to prepare for reading by painting with large brushes, doing jig-saw puzzles, arranging large building blocks, or writing numbers. Preparation for reading can be done more directly with written language.

Having established that printed forms are the remedial media, one can then allow that simplification, right down to the parts of the letters, may at times be required for some children. However, *the larger the chunks of printed language the child can work with, the more quickly he learns*, and the richer the network of meanings he can use. We should only dwell on detail long enough for the child to discover its existence and then encourage the use of it in isolation only when absolutely necessary. As a reader the child will use detail within and as a part of a pattern of cues or stimuli. The relationships of details to patterns in reading have often been destroyed by our methods of instruction. It is so easy for us as teachers, or for the designers of reading materials, to achieve that destruction.

There have been many attempts to match teaching methods to the strengths of groups of children. The child with good visual perception is said to benefit from sight-word methods; the child with good auditory perception is thought to make better progress on phonic methods. One author writes: 'Children are physiologically oriented to visual or auditory learning.' Another says, 'Teaching phonics as a relatively "pure" form will place a child at a disadvantage if he is delayed in auditory perceptual ability'! Such instruction would place all children at a severe disadvantage; they would have to learn by themselves many skills that their teachers were not teaching, if they were to become successful readers.

Such matching attempts are simplistic, for English is a complex linguistic system. The way to use a child's strengths and improve his weaknesses is not to work on one or the other but to design the tasks so that he practises the weakness with the aid of his strong abilities. Rather than take sides on reading methods which deal either with sounds that are synthesised or with sentences which are analysed,

> ...it is appropriate to select reading texts which are simple and yet retain the full power of semantic and syntactic richness, helping the child to apply his strong speaking abilities to their analysis on any level of language.

Close observation of a child's weaknesses will be needed because he will depend on the teacher to structure the task in simple steps to avoid the accumulation of confusions. For one child the structuring may be in the visual perception area. For another it may be in sentence patterns. For a third it may be in the discrimination of sound sequences. For a fourth it may be in directional learning. It is most likely to be in the bringing together of all these ways of responding as the reader works sequentially through a text.

It therefore seems appropriate to seek diagnosis of those aspects of the reading process which are weak in a particular child soon after he has entered instruction. The Observation Survey has been used to provide such information for children taught in very different programmes for beginning reading (in New Zealand, Scotland, Australia and the United States). Children in different programmes of instruction do not score in similar ways but the Observation Survey provides a framework within which early reading behaviour can be explored irrespective of the method of instruction. What

will vary from programme to programme will be the typical scores on the tests of the Survey after a fixed time in instruction.

In what follows there is only slight emphasis on scores and quantifying progress. The real value of the Observation Survey is to uncover what a particular child controls and what operations (see below) and items he could be taught next.

Reading instruction often focuses on items of knowledge, words, letters and sounds. Most children respond to this teaching in active ways. They search for links between the items and they relate new discoveries to old knowledge. They operate on print as Piaget's children operate on problems, searching for relationships which order the complexity of print and therefore simplify it.

The end-point of *early* instruction has been reached when children have a self-extending system of literacy behaviours and learn more about reading every time they read, independent of instruction. When they read texts of appropriate difficulty for their present skills, using their knowledge of oral and written language and their knowledge of the world, they use a set of operations or strategies 'in their heads' which are just adequate for reading the more difficult bits of the text. In the process they engage in 'reading work', a deliberate effort to solve new problems with familiar information and procedures. They notice new things about words, and constructively link these things to both their knowledge of the world around them, and their knowledge of the printed language gained in their short history of successful reading of simple books. The process is progressive and accumulative. The newly noticed feature(s) of print, worked upon today, becomes the reference point for another encounter in a few days. 'Television' as a new word becomes a reference point for 'telephone' in a subsequent text. Children are working on two theories — what Smith (1978) calls their theory of the world and what will make sense, and a second theory of how written language is created. They are testing these two theories and changing them successively as they read more books.

In the Observation Survey an emphasis will be placed on the operations or strategies that are used in reading, rather than on test scores or on disabilities.

> The terms *operation* or *strategy* are used for mental activities initiated by the child to get messages from a text.

1   A child may have the necessary abilities but may not have learned how to use those abilities in reading. He will not be observed to use helpful strategies. *He must learn how to work effectively with the information in print.*

2   Or a child may have made insufficient development in one ability area (say, motor coordination) to acquire the required strategy (say, directional behaviour) without special help. *He must learn how to ... in spite of ...*

3   Again, a child may have items of knowledge about letters and sounds and words but be unable to relate one to the other, to employ one as a cross-check on the other, or to get to the messages in print. He is unable to use his knowledge in the service of getting to the messages. *He must learn how to check on his own learning ... and how to orchestrate different ways of responding to complete a smooth message-getting process.*

In any of these instances the task for the reading/writing programme is to get the child to learn to use any and all of the strategies or operations that are necessary to read texts of a given level of difficulty.

There is an important assumption in this approach. Given a knowledge of some items, and a *strategy* which can be applied to similar items to extract messages, the child then has a general way of approaching new items. We do not need to teach him the total inventory of items. Using the strategies will lead the reader to the assimilation of new items of knowledge. Strategies for problem solving novel features of print are an important part of a self-extending system.

An example may help to clarify this important concept. Teachers through the years have taught children the relationship of letters and sounds. They have, traditionally, shown letters and given children opportunities to associate sounds with those letters. There seemed to be an obvious need to help the child to translate the letters in his book into the sounds of spoken words. And, in some vague way, this also helped the child in his spelling and story writing.

In our studies of children after one year of instruction we found children at risk in reading who could give the sounds of letters but who found it impossible to hear the sound sequences in the words they spoke. They could go *from letters to sounds* but they were unable to check whether they were right or not because they could not hear the sound sequence in the words they spoke. They were unable to go *from sounds to letters*. Being able to carry out the first operation, letters to sounds, probably leads easily to its inverse for many children but for some of our children at risk one strategy did not imply the other.

After six months of special tutoring Tony's progress report at the age of 6:3 (see below) emphasises not the item gains (in Letter Identification or Reading Vocabulary) but the actions or operations that he can initiate. He can analyse some initial sounds in words, uses language cues, has a good locating response, checks his predictions and has a high self-correction rate.

Tony

- (aged 5:9) has some early concepts about directionality and one-to-one correspondence but his low letter identification score and nil scores on word tests mean that he has no visual signposts with which to check his fluent book language.
- (aged 6:0) has made only slight progress in the visual area. In reading patterned text, he relies heavily on language prediction from picture clues and good memory for text, with very little use of visual information. His self-correction behaviour is almost nil, the two corrections made were on the basis of known words.
- (aged 6:3) identifies 37/54 letter symbols, has started accumulating a reading and writing vocabulary and can analyse some initial sounds in words. In reading unpatterned text, he uses language cues, a good locating response, known reading vocabulary and some initial sounds to check his predictions. He has a high self-correction rate.

An approach to literacy learning which emphasises the acquisition of reading strategies bypasses questions of reading ages and learning disabilities. It demands the recording of what the child does, on texts of specified difficulty; it refers to the strengths and weaknesses of his strategies, and compares these with a model of the strategies used by children who make satisfactory progress in reading. It assumes that the learner gradually constructs a network of strategies which make up a self-extending system, allowing the learner to continue to learn to read by reading, and learn to write by writing.

4 TAKING RUNNING RECORDS OF READING TEXTS

This Observation Survey which I have recommended for use with children during their first year of school, as the need arises, is one way of escaping from the problems of readiness tests. The observation tasks discussed in this chapter and the next can be used to supplement the observations that teachers make as they work alongside children. These include:

- running records
- letter identification
- concepts about print
- word tests
- writing
- hearing sounds in words (dictation).

The observation tasks provide for a standard or repeatable way of comparing a child's performance over a period of time. The tasks enable teachers to observe children at work noting all their responses (successful and unsuccessful). Teachers can then summarise where children are in their understanding of written language and can use this as the foundation for what those children are ready to learn next. *In complex learning, what is already known provides the learner with a useful context within which to embed new learning.*

At some point, not later than the end of the first year at school, it is a good idea to get a profile of learners on all these observation tasks because they cover areas of learning which underpin successful progress in reading and writing. If time does not permit individual testing of a whole class then the teacher should decide which children she knows are reading and writing well, and use the whole set of observation tasks with the lower half of her class. This will give her more information than giving only half the measures to all pupils in her class.

A set of standard observation procedures for recording reading and writing behaviours has a number of classroom applications. Various kinds of bias can affect

such observations (see page 7) and it is necessary to make our interpretations as reliable as we can. This can be achieved by:

- using standard procedures
- becoming skilled at applying the procedures
- using a wide range of observations which can be checked one against the other.

The procedures described in Chapters 4 and 5 have been found useful for monitoring the progress of beginning readers and writers, and for detecting reading difficulties early. In the light of recent theoretical discussions of literacy learning it is desirable:

- to observe precisely what children are saying and doing
- to use tasks that are close to the learning tasks of the classroom (rather than standardised tests of reading or spelling)
- to observe what children have been able to learn (not what they have *not* been able to learn)
- to discover what reading behaviours they should now be taught from an analysis of performance as they read, not from pictorial or puzzle material or from normative scores
- to shift the child's reading behaviour from less adequate to more adequate responding, by training on reading tasks (on-task activities) rather than training 'skills' like visual perception or auditory discrimination (off-task activities) in the hope that such training might facilitate learning to read and write.

In this Observation Survey several different types of observation tasks are described. *No one task is satisfactory on its own*. Teachers are advised to apply as many as possible to the children for whom important instructional decisions must be made. Reducing the scope of our observations increases the risk that we will make erroneous interpretations. For example, the Concepts About Print test should not be used in isolation because it assesses only one aspect of early reading behaviours. In research studies it is an excellent predictor of subsequent reading progress, but it tells the teacher nothing about the child's knowledge of letters, or of words, or of writing, or of letter-sound relationships. In a profile of scores a child may be high on concepts about print and low on letters and word knowledge, or vice versa. In the early stages of literacy learning no single measure is going to inform the teacher. The child's learning is progressing on several fronts at the same time, and the teacher must know about the spurts and lags in different knowledge areas in order to make the most of her teaching interactions with a particular child.

And without an observation of the child's attempts at text reading or writing the teacher has no idea of how the child is managing to bring some of this rather isolated knowledge to bear on more holistic literacy tasks. So text reading and text writing become of focal interest to the teacher.

To teach yourself something about these procedures it would be a good idea to make three case studies. Select children who are in the first year of formal instruction and who are making some progress but are clearly finding the task challenging. Try out the procedures on these children, score and analyse the results and summarise what you have observed. If you select children with a lot of literacy knowledge as your case studies you will leave yourself less to learn from the exercise. On the other hand, you need to become familiar with the tasks before you give them to a child with little literacy knowledge. So practise on an average child in the first year of formal instruction.

Although these tasks can be used productively to observe older failing readers it is important to first gain skill in administration and interpretation of the Observation Survey on the young children for whom it was designed.

WHICH CHILDREN NEED THESE DETAILED OBSERVATIONS?

After taking into account the opportunities a particular child has had to learn about literacy before he came to school, and the time a child has been at school, select for further study those about whom you feel you need more information, especially those who are not making good progress. This should occur before the end of the first

year of instruction. In New Zealand schools this occurs on or around the child's sixth birthday (6:0), after the child has been at school one year. This survey will probably include 30 to 50 percent of the class. The time required for such a survey is an investment in successful progress in literacy learning because more effective teaching can come from it. School principals must become convinced of this preventive need so that they accept the importance of giving time to this kind of assessment.

There are several reasons why the sixth birthday seems a better checkpoint than the end of the school year in New Zealand schools. This would stagger the testing load throughout the year and would therefore ensure more individual consideration for each child. At any one time in the year a complete survey of all children would be time-consuming and the range of tests applied would tend to be reduced. Children could be selected for observation surveys according to the level of puzzlement of their teacher. When she is puzzled by the child's responses a teacher needs more information; if the child is learning rapidly and progressing well, she apparently has the information she needs to be an effective teacher for that child.

In addition to these intermittent observations by teachers a school may well decide, as a matter of policy, to have a systematic check of those children falling in the lower half of the class at the end of the first year of instruction.

A school with a large number of children in this age-group could use the Observation Survey with a random sample of its children to watch how learning from the beginning of one year changes the performance of the pupils by, say, the end of the school year. Notice that for this purpose only a *sample* of pupils need be tested, and in this case the purpose is not to guide the learning of individual pupils.

WHAT TO CAPTURE IN YOUR RECORDS

The observations of literacy behaviours which are described in this book are controlled, and not casual. Perfect performance is easy to record and that is what traditional assessment has been concerned with. When the performance is less than perfect there are opportunities to record the work done by the child as he tries to puzzle it out. This reveals something of the processes by which the child monitors and corrects his own performance.

When he encounters something new we can observe how he approaches the novel thing, and what he learns from the encounter.

For example, one thing that readers do as they read is correct some of the errors without any prompting. Observing this we must ask 'How can this be? Why does the child do that?' One might reply, 'It's something in his memory.' But when one asks what cues the child might have been using, consistencies are found. The child gathers up cues from the structure of the sentence, or the meaning of the message, or the visual cues of the letters or letter order. We can infer from the kinds of errors and self-corrections that children make, together with their comments, much of what they are attending to. The learning work which goes on at these moments of choosing between possible responses is captured in a running record of reading, or the child's independent effort to write a story.

As the child learns to talk in the preschool years he produces many ungrammatical sentences and uses words in unusual ways. Researchers have recorded that the errors of the two-year-old disappear as he gains more control over language, but they report new kinds of errors in the three-year-old who is trying new things. This can be seen in early literacy learning too. Partially correct responses do not disappear because the child is always trying new things; gaining control over some simple responses frees the child to make partially correct attempts in some new area of learning. And this continues throughout his schooling and into adulthood.

So the observation records should contain all the behaviours the child produces on the task, including the comments he makes about what he is doing!

OBSERVING TEXT READING BEHAVIOUR WITH RUNNING RECORDS

Stories to assess text reading would best be selected from readily available reading materials used within the regular classroom programme.

Text difficulty and text type

Throughout schooling reading progress is indicated by satisfactory reading of increasingly difficult texts. New strategies are developed by the reader to cope with increase in the difficulty level of the text when complexities are introduced like multisyllabic words or literary forms of sentence structure or new kinds of texts (genres).

When the text is close to the natural language of the young child the frequently occurring words of English are read over and over again and the combinations of sounds typically found in English words used by young children occur in their natural frequencies. These frequencies are the naturally occurring equivalents of vocabulary and letter-sound controls imposed by basal series authors in the past on many texts for young readers. Their existence in all texts seems to have been overlooked by the advocates of texts with controlled vocabulary.

If the young child is moving up through texts of increasing levels of difficulty which use child-like language and which exercise a minimum of control over structures and vocabulary, and if he achieves 90 to 95 percent accuracy by the end of a normal teaching contact with that material, then he will be getting the opportunity to practise both the words he needs to learn and the clusters of sounds in those words that will help him to analyse new words.

The 'ifs' in the last paragraph imply that we must get reliable measures of how well children read their books because this is important information for planning day-to-day instruction. Running records, described below, have proved useful in this respect.

The pivotal observation among all these observation tasks, without which all others could be misleading, is *a running record of text reading*. Accounts of how teachers use these in their classroom activities are found in *Reading in the Junior Classes* (Department of Education, 1985). The running record is similar to Goodman and Burke's miscue analysis (1972) but it is particularly useful for the teacher in her day-to-day activities of the classroom, especially if she teaches young children. Running records are taken without marking a prepared script. They may be done on any piece of paper. With practice teachers can take a running record at any time, anywhere, on any text because the behaviour of the moment needs to be captured, and because the opportunity arises. Teachers do not need a tape-recorder. They do not have to carry out a long subsequent analysis of the record, and they do not need a technical knowledge of linguistic concepts to derive benefit from the record.

Classroom teachers can use running records for instructional purposes (see Department of Education, 1985) to guide them in their decisions about any of the following:

- the evaluation of text difficulty
- the grouping of children

- the acceleration of a child
- monitoring progress of children
- allowing different children to move through different books at different speeds while keeping track of (and records of) individual progress
- observing particular difficulties in particular children.

For critical decisions such as those made in a survey to find the children having most difficulty, to provide special and supplementary assistance, to make decisions about promotion, or to inform a psychologist of the child's progress it would be wise to obtain running records on materials from at least three levels of difficulty:

- an easy text (95 to 100 percent correct)
- an instructional text (90 to 94 percent correct)
- a hard text (80 to 89 percent correct).

In practice teachers in New Zealand have assumed that an easy text was one which the child had read successfully in the past (or one very like it); an instructional text was one which had already been introduced to the child so that he was somewhat familiar with the message and meanings of the story but had to engage in reading work and problem-solving to read the text at the required accuracy level (90 percent or above); and the hard book may have been introduced or may be an unseen text which one suspects the child will read less well and with which he will have some difficulty reaching the 90 percent accuracy level. The reason for using a 'seen' text for the instructional level record is that we want to see how well the reader orchestrates the various kinds of reading behaviours he controls, given that his reading is being guided by the meaningfulness of the text. The 'seen' text ensures that the child understands the messages of the text and meaningfulness will guide the reading.

This assumes that there is some gradient of difficulty in the texts used for reading in the school's programme, even if the children are learning to read from story books. The current book (or a selection from that book) will usually provide the instructional level. These three

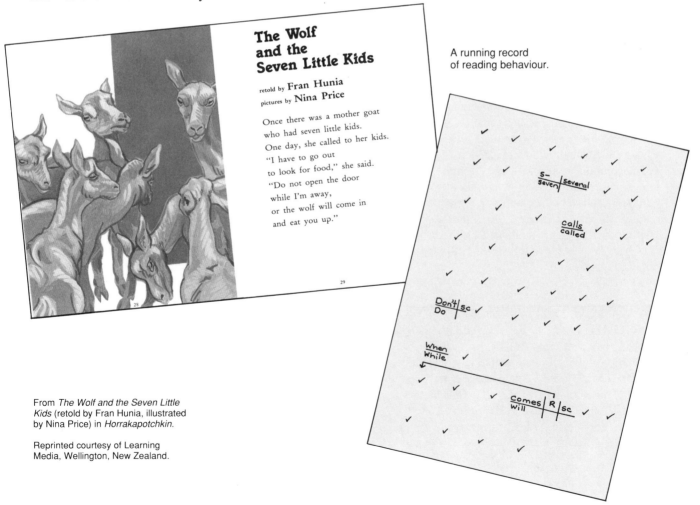

The Wolf and the Seven Little Kids

retold by **Fran Hunia**
pictures by **Nina Price**

Once there was a mother goat
who had seven little kids.
One day, she called to her kids.
"I have to go out
to look for food," she said.
"Do not open the door
while I'm away,
or the wolf will come in
and eat you up."

A running record of reading behaviour.

From *The Wolf and the Seven Little Kids* (retold by Fran Hunia, illustrated by Nina Price) in *Horrakapotchkin*.

Reprinted courtesy of Learning Media, Wellington, New Zealand.

samples on three levels of difficulty provide valuable insights into

- how the reader *orchestrates effective reading* (on the easier materials)
- how *processing and problem-solving* can be done (on instructional texts)
- and how and when *effective processing breaks down* (on the more difficult materials).

The classroom teacher will probably choose text materials that are part of her everyday programme. A visitor to the school (such as a reading adviser, a speech therapist or a school psychologist) should ask the class teacher for the book the child is working on at present, and for her suggestions about texts that are *just a little* harder or easier in her programme.

However, if there are reasons why such judgements are not easily made, for example because the class does not use any recognisably graded sets of materials, or a teacher new to this class level has no sense of a gradient of difficulty in the stories being read, then the teacher or observer may wish to use a standard set of graded paragraphs. From these the observer can select paragraphs which provide evidence of reading skills on three levels of difficulty which reveal strengths, processing and difficulties.

To take good records of reading behaviour teachers must be well trained. Six teachers taking and scoring the same record should get the same results. One teacher reading another teacher's record should be able to replay what a child actually said and did.

The running record on page 23 shows a child sampling and predicting (intelligently but incorrectly) 'several', and later returning and self-correcting. Note that only a plural determiner, 'several', was considered possible before a plural noun, 'kids'. Here the child was using a knowledge of syntactic, as well as graphophonic, cues.

LEARNING TO TAKE A RUNNING RECORD

Learning to take a running record can unsettle teachers. Those who are used to standardised tests and norms question the simplicity of the behaviour records, and so do people who do not like standardised testing.

There is not a lot to learn before you begin taking a running record, just a few conventions. There is no reason to study a new set of concepts or understand some-

thing new about the reading process. The first step is a matter of action. You set yourself the task of recording everything that a child says and does as he tries to read the book you have chosen. Once you begin such recording, and after about two hours of initial practice, no matter how much you might be missing, you have made a good start. The more you take the records the more you will notice about children's behaviour. It is not a case of knowing everything first and then applying it. Try yourself out and you will begin to notice a few things that you have not noticed before. Practise some more and you will notice more. As your ear becomes tuned-in to reading behaviours and you gain control over the recording conventions your records will become more and more reliable.

I had been teaching reading and remedial reading for many years when I began my research on emergent reading behaviour. I am still humble about the fact that I had never noticed self-correction behaviour until I started recording everything that children were doing. It was then I found that I had been missing something that was very important.

What we are observing and recording is not something that is peculiar to the child who is learning to read. If I take some adult volunteers and ask them to read some ordinary everyday reading materials their reading behaviour can be broken down so that we can observe the same kinds of behaviour that occur in children's reading. A smudgy carbon copy, a poor fax copy, a Churchill speech in i.t.a., a newspaper extract with misprints where the lines have been misplaced, or a very difficult scientific or medical text will break down the reading behaviours of competent adults and one can observe self-correction, word-by-word reading and even the use of a pointing finger to locate themselves on the text. Everybody's reading behaviour can be broken down under difficulties.

Make a record of each child reading his three little books or book selections. Use ticks for each correct response and record every error in full. A sample reading of 100 to 200 words from each text is required. This should take about 10 minutes. At the early reading level when the child is reading the very simplest texts the number of words may fall below 100 but if three texts are attempted (selected from caption books or first readers or teacher-made books or child-dictated text) this will be satisfactory even though the extracts themselves are short.

A suggested format for a Running Record Sheet can be found on page 25, and procedures for calculating accuracy and self-correction rates are on page 39.

RUNNING RECORD SHEET

Name: _____ Date: _____ D. of B.: _____ Age: ____ yrs ____ mths

School: _____ Recorder: _____

Text Titles	Running words Error	Error rate	Accuracy	Self-correction rate
1. Easy _____	_____	1: _____	_____ %	1: _____
2. Instructional _____	_____	1: _____	_____ %	1: _____
3. Hard _____	_____	1: _____	_____ %	1: _____

Directional movement _____

Analysis of Errors and Self-corrections
Information used or neglected [Meaning (M) Structure or Syntax (S) Visual (V)]

Easy _____

Instructional _____

_____

Hard _____

_____

Cross-checking on information (Note that this behaviour changes over time)

_____

_____ Analysis of Errors and Self-corrections
(see *Observation Survey* pages 30–32)

Page		E	SC	Information used E MSV	SC MSV

Page		E	SC	Information used	
				E MSV	SC MSV

SOME CONVENTIONS USED FOR RECORDING

1 Mark every word read correctly with a tick (or check). A record of the first five pages of the 'Ready to Read' (1963) book *Early in the Morning* that was 100 percent correct would look like this. (The lines indicate page breaks.)

Bill is asleep.	✓	✓	✓
'Wake up, Bill,'	✓	✓	✓
said Peter.	✓	✓	
Sally is asleep.	✓	✓	✓
'Wake up, Sally,'	✓	✓	✓
said Mother.	✓	✓	
Father is shaving.	✓	✓	✓

2 Record a wrong response with the text under it.

Child: *home*
Text: house   [One error]

3 If a child tries several times to read a word, record all his trials.

Child: *here* | *h—* | *home*
Text: house | | [One error]

Child: *h—* | *ho—* | *home*
Text: home | | [No error]

4 If a child succeeds in correcting a previous error this is recorded as 'self-correction' (written SC). Note that example **3** did not result in a self-correction.

Child: *where* | *when* | SC
Text: were | | [No error]

5 If no response is given to a word it is recorded with a dash. Insertion of a word is recorded over a dash.

No response   Insertion

Child: —   *Child:* *here*
                                              ⎤ In each case
Text: house   Text: —   ⎦ one error

6 If the child baulks, unable to proceed because he is aware he has made an error and cannot correct it,

or because he cannot attempt the next word, he is told the word (written T).

Child: *home* |
Text: house | T   [One error]

7 An appeal for help (A) from the child is turned back to the child for further effort before using T as in **6** above. Say 'You try it'.

Child: — | A | *here*
Text: house | — | T   [One error]

8 Sometimes the child gets into a state of confusion and it is necessary to extricate him. The most detached method of doing this is to say 'Try that again', marking TTA on the record. This would not involve any teaching, but the teacher may indicate where the child should begin again.

   It is a good idea to put square brackets around the first set of muddled behaviour, enter the TTA, remember to count that as one error only (see page 29), and then begin a fresh record of the problem text. An example of this recording would be:

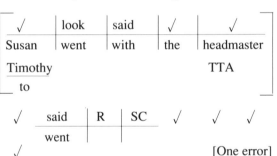

9 Repetition (R) is not counted as error behaviour. Sometimes it is used to confirm a previous attempt. Often it results in self-correction. It is useful to record it as it often indicates how much sorting out the child is doing. 'R', standing for repetition, is used to indicate repetition of a word, with R_2 or R_3 indicating the number of repetitions. If the child goes back over a group of words, or returns to the beginning of the line or sentence in his repetition, the point to which he returns is shown by an arrow.

Child: Here is the home | R | SC
Text: Here is the house | | [No error]

10 Sometimes the child re-reads the text (repetition) and corrects some but not all errors. The following example shows the recording of this behaviour.

Child: a | SC | *house* R   [One error]
Text: the | | home   [One SC]

11 Directional attack on the printed text is recorded by telling the child to 'Read it with your finger'.

Left to right   L ⟶ R
Right to left   L ⟵ R
Snaking
Bottom to top   B ⟶ T

For special purposes teachers or researchers may wish to develop their own conventions for scoring other behaviours which they notice. Some behaviours may be specific to, or important for, a particular teaching programme. For example, pausing can be recorded by a slash, /. Some researchers who have been concerned with the length of pausing have used a convention borrowed from linguistics which allows for pauses of four different lengths. These are quickly recorded as

/   //   ⫽   #

I would caution against attention to pausing unless there is a special reason for wishing to record it. *In research studies it has not yet yielded clear messages about the reading process* (Clay and Imlach, 1971). It adds little to the teacher's interpretation of her record and may cause confusion. Pausing behaviour is sensitive to the instructional programme and may have been induced by the ways in which children are being taught. Pauses do not necessarily mean that 'reading work' (as I discuss this concept in Clay, 1991), is taking place. *It would be important not to read things into a record of pausing interpretations for which there was no other evidence.*

A running record from a child who is making many errors is harder to take and score but the rule is to record all behaviour, and analyse objectively what is recorded.

Reliability
Taped recordings of such reading observations taken from four children over the period of one year were available and were used to check on the reliability of such records (0.98 for error scoring and 0.68 for self-correction scoring, Clay, 1966).

A number of trends became obvious during these reliability tests.

- For beginning readers, observers can take running records which give reliable accuracy scores with a small amount of training.
- The effect of poor observation is to reduce the number of errors recorded and increase the accuracy rate. As the observer's skill in recording at speed increases, so the error scores tend to rise.
- To record all error behaviour in full, as against only tallying its occurrence, takes much more practice (but provides more evidence of the child's strategies).
- Observations for poor readers require longer training to reach agreement on scoring standards because of the complex error behaviour.
- Information is lost in the taped observation, especially motor behaviour and visual survey, but observation of vocal behaviour tends to be improved.
- Reliability probably drops as reading accuracy level falls because there is more error behaviour to be recorded in the same time span.

For research work the most reliable records would be obtained by scoring an observation immediately following its manual recording, and rechecking immediately with a taped observation.

ANALYSING THE READING RECORD

From the running record of reading behaviour containing all the child's behaviour on his current book, consider what is happening as the child reads.

Some conventions for scoring the records
In counting the number of errors, some arbitrary decisions must be made but the following have been found workable.

1 Credit the child with any correct or corrected words.

Child: *to*   *the*   *shops*
Text: for   the   bread
Score: ✗   ✓   ✗   [Two errors]

2 There is no penalty for trials which are eventually correct.

A *Child*: *want* | *won't* | *went* | SC
    Text: went | | | [No error]
    Score: —   —   ✓   [One SC]

B

Child:	where	we	when	were	SC
Text:	were				[No error]
Score:	—	—	—	√	[One SC]

3 Insertions add errors so that a child can have more errors than there are words in a line.

Child:	The	train	went	toot,	toot,	toot
Text:	The	little	engine	sighed		
Score:	√	×	×	×	×	×
						[Five errors]

4 However, the child cannot receive a minus score for a page. The lowest page score is 0.

5 *Omissions.* If a line or sentence is omitted each word is counted as an error.

If pages are omitted (perhaps because two pages were turned together) they are not counted as errors. Note that in this case, the number of words on the omitted pages must be deducted from the Running Words Total before calculation.

6 *Repeated errors.* If the child makes an error (e.g., 'run' for 'ran') and then substitutes this word repeatedly, it counts as an error every time; but substitution of a proper name (e.g., 'Mary' for 'Molly') is counted only the first time.

7 *Multiple errors and self-correction.* If a child makes two or more errors (e.g., reads a phrase wrongly) each word is an error. If he then corrects all these errors each corrected word is a self-correction.

8 *Broken words.* Where a word is pronounced as two words (e.g., a/way) even when this is backed up by pointing as if it were two words, this is regarded as an error of pronunciation, not as a reading error unless what is said is matched to a different word. Such things as 'pitcher' for 'picture' and 'gonna' for 'going to' are counted as correct.

9 *Inventions* defeat the system. When the young child is creatively producing his own version of the story the scoring system finally breaks down and the judgement 'inventing' is recorded for that page, story or book.

10 *'Try that again'.* When the child is in a tangle this instruction, which does not involve teaching, can

be given. It counts as one error and only the second attempt is scored (see page 27).

11 *Fewest errors.* If there are alternate ways of scoring responses a general principle is to choose the method that gives the *fewest* possible errors as in B below.

A

Child:	We	went	for	the	bread			
Text:	You	went	to	the	shop	for	the	bread
Score:	×	√	×	√	×	×	×	×
								[Six errors]

B

Child:	We	went				for	the	bread
Text:	You	went	to	the	shop	for	the	bread
Score:	×	√	×	×	×	√	√	√
								[Four errors]

Check directional movement

A check on the visual survey being carried out by the reader is needed. Select a few lines of text during the reading and ask the child to 'Read this (part/page) with your finger'. A brief observation will suffice, if all is well. More use of pointing should be observed if this is necessary (for the observer to understand what the child is doing). While pointing may not be a desirable teaching instruction it is a necessary one for the observer to elicit evidence of directional movement. Record which hand was used, on which page, and the direction of movement.

In a study of children's early learning of directional movement across English texts a common progression was noted (Clay, 1982). There was an early period of confusion as the children tried to orient to the spatial characteristics of the open book. Then there was a period when the child seemed to prefer to use a particular hand for pointing to any text. Finally a more flexible set of behaviours emerged when the child could use either hand on either page without having to pay much attention to direction. As these stages were worked through, sometimes rapidly and sometimes over several months, lapses from directional behaviours were observed. Children might go from right to left or even from bottom to top. Left- and right-handed children showed similar kinds of behaviours.

Three groups of children have difficulty as beginning readers in disciplining their behaviour within the directional constraints of written language.

• The first group are children who have poor motor coordination or who are inattentive to where their bodies are and how they are arranging their movements.

- The second group are fast-reacting, impulsive children who act before they think and who have great difficulty in governing their responses within any constraints. They can very readily settle into undesirable patterns of responding.
- A third group of beginners at risk are those who do not like to try because they might make a mistake.

The development of directional behaviour involves exploring two-dimensional space, and discovering how to behave correctly within the constraints of the printer's code. Children need to be risk-takers. Children who are too tense, inhibited or timid, or afraid to be wrong may be reluctant to try out a range of directional behaviour. Consequently they take longer to learn to discard the poor responses and retain the good ones.

The technique of asking a child to 'Read it with your finger' will only reveal directional behaviour on the gross schema of line scanning. Beyond this there is some very important visual perception learning to be done. It relates to the scanning of letters and clusters of letters. There are further important orientation behaviours to be learned which involve what the eyes are attending to, and in what order. These orientation behaviours will not be picked up in observations of pointing behaviour.

Record your observations and comments on directional movement on your Running Record Sheet (page 25). Any lapse from appropriate directional behaviour is important and should be noted. We are not concerned merely with the child who habitually moves in the wrong direction, but rather with the child who is not yet consistent, or in other words is still in the process of learning directional control. This is shown by lapses from correct directional behaviour from time to time.

Calculate the error rate

Compare the number of errors with the number of running words. Does the child read his book with one error in every five running words of text (which is not good) or is it more like one error in 20 running words (which is good)? Record results on the Running Record Sheet.

Calculate the percentage of errors (see Conversion Table page 39). If there is more than 10 percent of error in the record rate this is a 'hard' text for this child. (For the average child there is movement from 90 percent

accuracy when he is first promoted to a book to 95 percent or more as he completes his learning on that book.)

When children read a book with less than 90 percent accuracy it is difficult for them to judge for themselves whether their attempts at a word are good ones or poor ones. They need easier material which they can attempt at a rate of not more than one error in 10 words at the time they begin the new book. The reading text should use language that they can easily anticipate. In the very earliest stages it is sometimes necessary to repeat the text until children have almost memorised it, but not quite. Then it will come readily to the tip of the tongue. It is as if the words the child needs are stored in the depths of memory and have to be assisted to float to the surface. The child's own dictated stories provide good reading texts for young children for just this reason— the words and construction of the text should be readily recalled.

If the text is in a different style from that which the child usually reads, his error rate may increase because he is predicting from the baseline of old expectations which are inappropriate for the present text.

Error behaviour: What can we learn from this?

To read a continuous text the child must use a variety of skills held in delicate balance. Specific weaknesses or strengths can upset that balance. There are some questions about the errors for a particular child that can guide the teacher's analysis of the behaviour record (see also Clay, 1991). At this point attend only to the errors (and not the self-corrections).

Oral language skills

Are these good enough to make the reading of this text possible? (For instance, could the child repeat the sentences of the text if you asked him to, one by one?) Or, is his language so fluent that the coordination of visual perception and motor movement with language is difficult?

Speed of responding

The rate at which a child reads and the time spent on pausing and processing cues are in the young child poor indicators of progress. One child may read with the fluency of oral language but may be a poorer reader than another child who pauses and engages in much self-correction behaviour. At this particular stage in reading progress it is good for the child making average progress to be concerned about error and try to rectify error if possible. It is poor to maintain fluency and not to notice that one has made errors.

Fast responding can be an indication that language is dominating the reading process allowing for little visual search to take place.

What kinds of information does the child use?

To work out whether the child is responding to the different sources of information in print (and the different kinds of cues that could be used) you need to look at every error that the child makes and ask yourself 'Now what led the child to do (or say) that?' Try to work out whether the child was using information from:

- the meaning of the message
- the structure of the sentence
- something from the visual cues.

Firstly, consider only the behaviour up to the error.

- *Meaning*. Does the child use meaning (M)? If what he reads makes sense, even though it is inaccurate, then he is probably applying his knowledge of the world to his reading.
- *Structure*. Is what he said possible in an English sentence (S for syntactically appropriate)? If it is, his oral language is probably influencing his responding. If it is not, there may be two reasons. Perhaps his language skill is limited and his personal 'grammar' does not contain the structures used in his reading book. Or, if he is paying close attention to detail, or to word-by-word reading, he may not be allowing his control over English syntax to influence his choices.
- *Visual information*. Does he use visual information (V) from the letters and words or the layout of print?*
- *Word memory*. Does he read word by word as if recalling each word from a memory bank, unrelated to what has gone before? He may not realise that reading is like speaking, and that his language behaviour is a rich source of help in choosing correct reading responses.

It is misleading if the teacher looks for error behaviour selectively; one should analyse every error and count those that show attention to this or that kind of cue. We want to be able to conclude, on good evidence, that 'He pays more attention to visual cues than to meaning', or 'He is guided by structure and meaning but does not search for visual cues'. It is only when you go to the trouble of analysing *all the errors* that you get quality information about the way the reader is working on print.

When teachers are familiar with taking running records they may want to include error analysis on the record form. They can write M for meaning, S for structure and V for visual cues on the form and record, by circling which cues the child was using. (See Running Record Sheet, page 25.) Notice that what you are recording in this case is your best guess: *you cannot know what cues the child used*. A record may show one, two or three types of cues used on any one error. If you write M S V alongside each error and circle the cues you think the child used, the uncircled letters will then show the cues neglected.

You have considered the errors first, and you know what cues *up to that error* the child was using.

Enter comments on the Analysis of Errors and Self-corrections (Running Record Sheet).

Cross-checking strategies

Now consider whether the child can check one kind of information with another.

Cross-checking is a tentative behaviour. It is not possible to be specific about it. One has a hunch that it is happening after observing the child. We must ask 'Is this child checking one kind of information against another?'

Cross-checking is most obvious when a child is not satisfied with a response for some reason. The child may make another attempt, or look back, or think again, or complain that a necessary letter is missing. Usually two sources of information are involved and one is checked against the other.

The child checks on the word which he read using one kind of information, by looking at a different kind of information. He uses meaning but complains that some letters are not there. He uses visual cues from letters but says that it doesn't make sense.

Some examples of this kind of behaviour are these.

- He can get both movement and language occurring together in a coordinated way, and knows when he has run out of words.
- He checks language prediction by looking at some letters.

---

*Whether the child is relating visual information to sounds (phonological information) or to orthography (information about spelling) is a refinement of using visual information not distinguished in this analysis at this time.

- He can hear the sounds in a word he speaks and checks whether the expected letters are there.
- After a wrong response a child can make another attempt at the word (searching).
- After a wrong response the child repeats the sentence, phrase or word, indicating he is aware and trying to get some additional information (repeating).
- After a wrong response the child makes a verbal comment about it, for example, 'No! That's not right!' (commenting on the mismatch).

It is useful to try to specify which two kinds of information the child is comparing. Usually cross-checking is reserved for describing early behaviours that suggest the child knows there are different kinds of information in print and that one kind can be compared with another kind and one expects all kinds to agree on the solution. Most of this behaviour becomes superseded by more deliberate and successful attempts to self-correct using multiple sources of information.

A child with outstanding memory for what he hears or with very fast language production often has difficulty in slowing up enough to enable him to learn the visual discriminations. Yet good readers search for cues from different sources which confirm a response. (See pages 9 to 11 and Clay, 1991 for further discussion of these reading behaviours.)

Self-correction

Now look at any self-correction behaviour in the running record. This occurs when the child discovers information in the text that tells him something is wrong. He is aware that a particular message is to be communicated and tries to discover this by using cues. Efficient self-correction behaviour is an important skill in good reading. Calculate the self-correction rate (see page 39). Even if the self-correction rate is low the prognosis is good, because self-correction does exist!

When analysing self-corrections for the information they can give about the child's processing of print, consider the error first. What kind of information was the child using up to the time when the error occurred? Think only of the information in the error substitution. Then, in a two-step process, consider what extra information the child used to get the self-correction. What extra information is in the self-correction that was not in the error? Enter on the Running Record Sheet in the second of the analysis columns headed SC (self-correction) all the sources of information probably being used in the self-correction. Write MSV alongside each self-correction and circle the cues you think the child used. Are cross-checking strategies evident in the self-correction analysis?

If self-correction is evident but inefficient it is still a good prognosis. Its absence in a record which contains errors is a danger sign. A child who is making errors and is not aware of this, or who makes no attempt to correct himself, is in difficulty. He is not aware of the need to read a precise message or he is not aware of the existence of cues, or he does not know how to use them, or he does not try to solve the problem. Self-correction rates vary greatly. This is because they are not absolute scores: they are always relative measures. They vary with text difficulty, with error rate, with accuracy, and with effort. They cannot be understood unless they are interpreted together with text difficulty and accuracy scores.

Two examples of self-correcting behaviours

I Linda was 5:9 when she was reading the book which gave rise to the example of reading behaviours on page 33. (It was not a very helpful book for her level of reading and it was a 'contrived text' [Clay, 1991] using controlled vocabulary.) You might think that she was a poor reader. Yet when you think about what is going on in this record, and how many things she is trying to do, and what kinds of cues she is testing out, you can see that she really is working hard to relate one kind of information to another. This is a very interesting record of her behaviour, showing how active she is in searching and checking. In time she must become more efficient at doing these things.

II The next example comes from a child who was able to engage in finding and correcting her own errors as she read, almost independently, with very little assistance from her teacher.

The teacher listened as the child read one or two self-chosen, easy books. The teacher said 'Read it with your finger.'

'Now it came out right,' the child said. 'I had enough words for each time I pointed.'

The teacher offered no assistance as the child re-read the book they had worked on together in a previous lesson. They continued with the reading until the child, puzzled, stopped. (The teacher had said nothing.)

'That didn't make any sense,' the child observed, repeating the beginning of the sentence, taking another look. Then, after a moment, the child reflected aloud,

AN EXAMPLE OF VERY COMPLICATED WORD-SOLVING AND SELF-CORRECTION BEHAVIOUR

Response to: **I like the swing.** **I shall get on it.** **The swing went up** **and down.** **It went . . .**	INTERPRETATION OF BEHAVIOUR		
	TRIES	DECIDES	REASONS
I like the swing	Correct		
I shall ke — get	Anticipates wrongly	Corrects	Letter cue?
off it — on it	Anticipates wrongly	Corrects	Meaning?
The swing will — No!	First letter cue	Rejects	Word form?
wa — want	Three letters similar	Rejects	Meaning?
won't (up) — No!	Structure cue 'The swing won't . . .' plus three letters	Rejects	Following structure 'won't up'?
will take	New idea	Rejects	One pattern for two responses
we — *wa — No*	A more analytical approach	Rejects	Sounds do not aid recall
(I get mixed up)		'I am confused'	There is always some cue that does not fit
(I'll read it again)	A new approach	Return to the line beginning	'A clean slate'
The swing want	It looks like 'want'	Rejects	Meaning?
won't up and down	It looks like 'won't'	Accepts	Fits letter and meaning cues and previous structure
It — (I get mixed up)	Recognises the same word	I am confused. Start again.	
It won't	Tries previous solution	Rejects	
went?	Tries correct sound 'e'	I do not recognise this word	There has been too much error
(I don't know that word)	Gives up	Appeals for help	No more ideas

'Oh, it's *away*. That makes sense.'

A little later the child shook her head and seemed uncertain. The teacher asked, 'Why did you stop?'

'I don't remember that word.'

'What word would make sense there?'

'*Bike*. But this word is longer. It's got to be bike. Oh! It's *bicycle*.'

Keeping records of change over time

Education is primarily concerned with change in the learning of individuals, yet educators rarely document change over time in individuals as they grow and learn. Perhaps the diversity among individuals in all characteristics from height, to habits, to school achievements, clouds the progress that each makes. But it is not difficult to collect evidence of change over time in school learning, particularly from young children at the beginning of formal education.

Two ways of recording individual progress over time in running records are shown below. In Rochelle's case the teacher grouped her books into approximate levels of

ROCHELLE'S PROGRESS ON BOOKS
TWO OBSERVATION POINTS

BOOK LEVEL	Time 1			BOOK LEVEL	Time 2	
9				. . .		
8	— *Playtime*	(hard)		. . .		
7	— *Going to School*	(instructional)		18		
6	— *The Escalator*	(easy)		17		
5				16		
4				15	— *Hungry Lambs*	(hard)
3				14	— *A Wet Morning*	(instructional)
2				13	— *The Pet Show*	(easy)
1				12		
0				11		
				10		

JOAN'S PROGRESS ON BOOKS

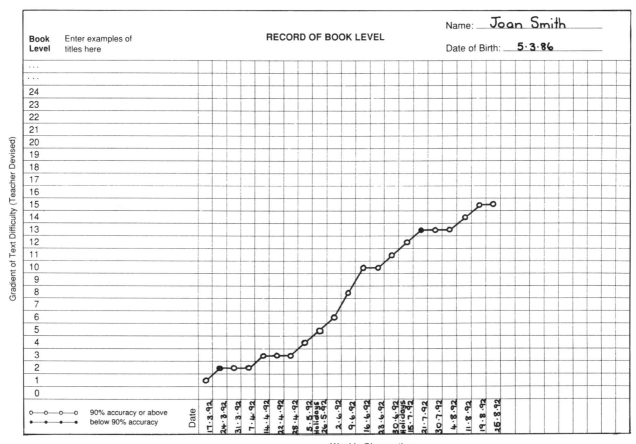

difficulty for her children. She placed these numbers on the left side of her sheet. Then, when she took her running records of Rochelle's reading on two occasions several months apart she entered in the name of the story which Rochelle read, and whether this story was easy, instructional or hard for Rochelle.

In Joan's case her teacher was keeping a very close record of her progress. This time the teacher used the Record of Book Level sheet on page 36. She entered the level of book difficulty on the left and entered the date of the observation along the horizontal line for the weekly observations she was taking. After hearing Joan read her current book she entered an open circle at the level of the one she considered her to be reading at an 'instructional' level (at 90 to 94 percent accuracy level). If no story was read at this level or better then the teacher had evidence that she had been making the task too difficult for Joan's current competencies and she entered a filled or black circle to alert her to her own error. Joan's record is a good one. Whenever her teacher

raises the challenge by introducing a more difficult text Joan is able to take the challenge and read at appropriate levels of accuracy.

A teacher may follow several children in this way, even though they were taught separately, using the same plotting procedures as she used for Joan but entering several children on one graph. This will not only give her a record of progress but also show many things about individual differences

- in the starting levels
- in the paths of progress
- in fast or slow 'take-off' in her programme
- in final or outcome levels.

She would be able to quickly identify any children who were working with texts that were too difficult for them, preventing them from working in the context of mostly correct reading (instructional level of 90 percent accuracy or above).

Teachers may follow the progress of several children in this way.

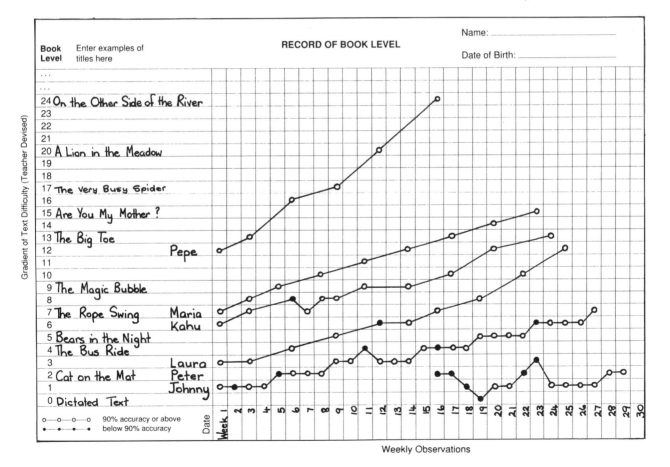

RECORD OF BOOK LEVEL

Name: _____

Date of Birth: _____

Book Level	Enter examples of titles here
⋮	
⋮	
24	
23	
22	
21	
20	
19	
18	
17	
16	
15	
14	
13	
12	
11	
10	
9	
8	
7	
6	
5	
4	
3	
2	
1	
0	
Date	

Gradient of Text Difficulty (Teacher Devised)

o—o—o—o 90% accuracy or above

•—•—•—• below 90% accuracy

Weekly Observations

Next we have two examples of what a teacher could learn from her running record about how pupils were trying to problem-solve text. Both records were taken in the first weeks of an early intervention programme.

- Child One shows dependence upon the visual information in text for his decision-making. He is paying some attention to sentence structure because his errors mostly belong to a class of words which could occur in the sentence (nouns and adjectives). However, he does not react to the lack of meaning in what he reads.

- Child Two is using language information and his errors all reflect the use of meaning and sentence structure in his decision-making. Child Two is not yet showing any awareness of a mismatch between his response and the visual information in the text.

Running records of the error behaviours displayed by two children at the beginning of a reading recovery programme.

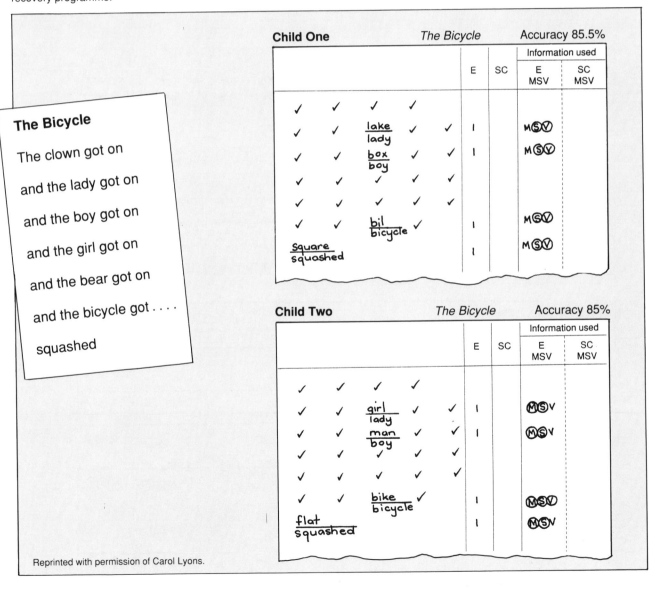

The Bicycle

The clown got on

and the lady got on

and the boy got on

and the girl got on

and the bear got on

and the bicycle got . . . .

squashed

Reprinted with permission of Carol Lyons.

A running record taken on the Running Record Sheet

RUNNING RECORD SHEET

Name: **Tina**   Date: **25·11·92**   D. of B.: **16·11·86** Age: **6** yrs **0** mths

School: **Fernwood**   Recorder: **V.S.**

Text Titles	Running words / Error	Error rate	Accuracy	Self-correction rate
1. Easy _____	_____	1: _____	_____ %	1: _____
2. Instructional _____	_____	1: _____	_____ %	1: _____
3. Hard **Dogs (Highgate/P.M.)(seen)**	$\frac{34}{4}$	1: **8·5**	**89** %	1: **2**

Directional movement __✓_____

Analysis of Errors and Self-corrections
Information used or neglected [Meaning (M) Structure or Syntax (S) Visual (V)]

Easy _____

Instructional _____

Hard **Meaning and structural cues are used predominantly for substitutions with some attention to visual information. Repetition with the use of visual cues led to three self-corrections.**
Cross checking on information (Note that this behaviour changes over time)
In two examples meaning and structure appear to be cross checked with visual information.

Analysis of Errors and Self-corrections
(see *Observation Survey* pages 30–32)

Page		E	SC	Information used E MSV	SC MSV
2	S— / Some T ✓ ✓ little / thin	2		M s Ⓥ / Ⓜ Ⓢ v	
3	✓ ✓ ✓ ✓				
4	✓ ✓ ✓ Scarey / growly	1		Ⓜ Ⓢ v	
5	✓ / ✓ dogs|R|sc / like ✓ ✓		1	Ⓜ Ⓢ v	M s Ⓥ
6	✓ ✓ ✓ ✓				
7	✓ / ✓ ✓ ✓ little | R | sc / small		1	Ⓜ Ⓢ v	M s Ⓥ
8	✓ / ✓ ✓ dog is | R | sc / dog's ✓ ✓		1	Ⓜ Ⓢ Ⓥ	Ⓜ Ⓢ Ⓥ
	✓ / ✓ ✓ biggest |R|A / cuddliest | | T ✓ ✓	1		Ⓜ Ⓢ v	
		4	3	6 6 2	0 1 3

Calculation and conversion table

Whether children are reading seen or unseen texts, most of their reading will contain errors. This is fortunate because it allows teachers to observe how children work on texts to problem-solve and monitor their own reading.

The Conversion Table provides for a quick conversion of error rate to a percentage accuracy score. This allows teachers to offer children texts which provide the support of a meaningful context within which to do their problem-solving.

CONVERSION TABLE

Error rate	Percent accuracy	
1 : 200	99.5	
1 : 100	99	
1 : 50	98	
1 : 35	97	
1 : 25	96	Good opportunities for teachers to observe children's 'reading work'.
1 : 20	95	
1 : 17	94	
1 : 14	93	
1 : 12.5	92	
1 : 11.75	91	
1 : 10	90	
1 : 9	89	
1 : 8	87.5	
1 : 7	85.5	The reader tends to lose the support of the meaning of the text.
1 : 6	83	
1 : 5	80	
1 : 4	75	
1 : 3	66	
1 : 2	50	

CALCULATIONS
(RW = Running words; E = Errors; SC = Self-corrections)

ERROR RATE	ACCURACY	SELF-CORRECTION RATE
$\dfrac{\text{Running words}}{\text{Errors}}$ e.g. $\dfrac{150}{15}$ = Ratio 1 : 10	$100 - \dfrac{E}{RW} \times \dfrac{100}{1}$ $100 - \dfrac{15}{150} \times \dfrac{100}{1}$ = 90%	$\dfrac{E + SC}{SC}$ $\dfrac{15 + 5}{5}$ = Ratio 1 : 4

Running records with older readers

Johnston (1992) has included running records in *Constructive Evaluation of Literate Activity*. Two chapters deal with 'Recording Oral Reading' and 'Making Sense of Records of Oral Reading'. In an appendix Johnston provides some practice examples and there is an accompanying audiotape for self-training in the procedures.

An analysis of error behaviour

Here are the graded paragraphs of the Neale Analysis of Reading Ability (Form B) administered to Brian, a boy aged 7:3 with very good reading strategies in his third year of instruction. For the text of the paragraphs refer to Neale (1958).

1

Paragraph one		
Running words	:	26
Accuracy	:	100%
Error rate	:	Nil
Self-correction rate	:	Nil
Repetition	:	Nil
Prompts	:	Nil
Comprehension	:	100%

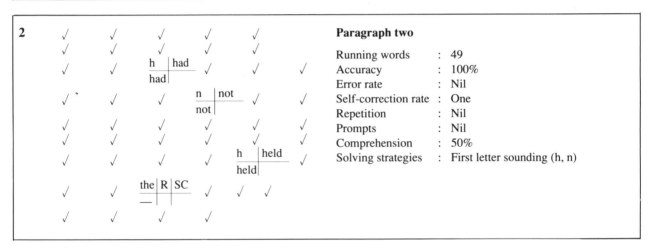

Paragraph two

Running words	:	49
Accuracy	:	100%
Error rate	:	Nil
Self-correction rate	:	One
Repetition	:	Nil
Prompts	:	Nil
Comprehension	:	50%
Solving strategies	:	First letter sounding (h, n)

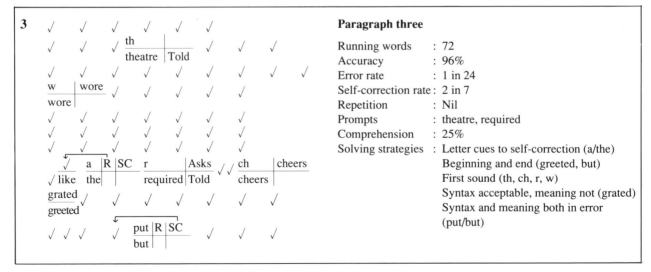

Paragraph three

Running words	:	72
Accuracy	:	96%
Error rate	:	1 in 24
Self-correction rate	:	2 in 7
Repetition	:	Nil
Prompts	:	theatre, required
Comprehension	:	25%
Solving strategies	:	Letter cues to self-correction (a/the)

Beginning and end (greeted, but)
First sound (th, ch, r, w)
Syntax acceptable, meaning not (grated)
Syntax and meaning both in error (put/but)

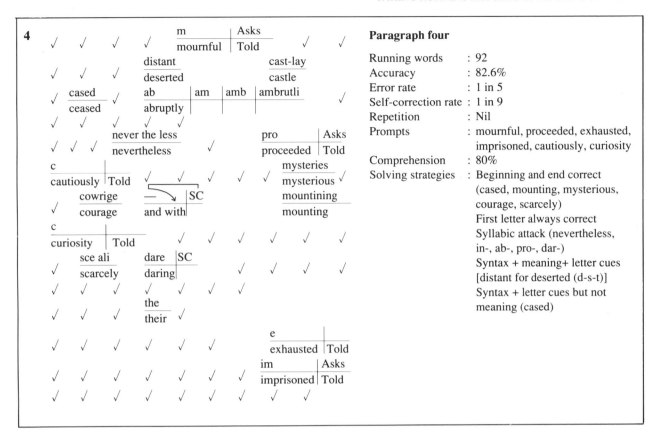

Paragraph four

Running words : 92
Accuracy : 82.6%
Error rate : 1 in 5
Self-correction rate : 1 in 9
Repetition : Nil
Prompts : mournful, proceeded, exhausted, imprisoned, cautiously, curiosity
Comprehension : 80%
Solving strategies : Beginning and end correct (cased, mounting, mysterious, courage, scarcely)
First letter always correct
Syllabic attack (nevertheless, in-, ab-, pro-, dar-)
Syntax + meaning+ letter cues [distant for deserted (d-s-t)]
Syntax + letter cues but not meaning (cased)

Scoring and analysis
In addition to standard scoring of the Neale Test these running records of reading behaviour made by a second year education student were described in the following way. (A summary table is on page 42.)

Descriptive comments *
Brian read word by word, staccato, at a fast pace. He ignored punctuation and paused at difficult words and the end of lines, losing meaning and sense. Intonation was flat and even with little variation.

In correcting himself Brian went back to the previous word but not to the beginning of the sentence or line.

*The author is indebted to the careful observation of Maris O'Rourke for this case study.

Brian used initial letters or clusters and last letters or clusters for cues. He did not use medial sounds, syllables or clusters as efficiently.

Recommendations
Although only seven years of age Brian has a reading age of nine years and this analysis of his reading of continuous text shows that two emphases typical of nine-year-old learning are required in Brian's programme. He could now develop a more consciously controlled syllabic attack, with attention to medial vowels and syllables. Meantime he should place more value on meaning by using punctuation cues, by phrasing, and by searching until the difficult word makes sense.

This may mean a temporary drop in fluency while syllabic attack and semantic checks are incorporated into his present patterns of reading behaviour.

FROM A RUNNING RECORD OF A SEVEN-YEAR-OLD USING TESTS FROM THE NEALE ANALYSIS OF READING ABILITY (1958)

PARAGRAPH	ONE	TWO	THREE	FOUR
Running words	26	49	72	92
Accuracy	100%	100%	96%	83%
Error rate	nil	nil	1:24	1:5
Self-correction rate	nil	(one)	1:3	1:9
Repetition	nil	nil	nil	nil
Prompts	nil	nil	theatre, required	mournful, proceeded exhausted, imprisoned cautiously, curiosity
Comprehension	100%	50%	25%	80%
Solving strategies	nil	first letters sounded (h,n)	**1** letter cues (a/the) **2** beginning and end (greeted, but) **3** first sound (th, ch, r, w) **4** syntax acceptable, meaning not (grated) **5** syntax + meaning both in error (put, but)	**1** beginning and end correct (cased, mounting, mysterious, courage, scarcely) **2** first letter always correct **3** syllabic attack (nevertheless, in-, ab-, pro-, dar-) **4** syntax + meaning + letter cues [distant for deserted (d-s-t)] **5** syntax + letter cues but not meaning (cased)

5 | OTHER OBSERVATION TASKS

The reader may wish to refer back to pages 20–21 of the general introduction to the Observation Survey before reading Chapter 5, noting in particular the warning that no one task is satisfactory as an assessment on its own.

LETTER IDENTIFICATION

What letters does the child know? Which letters can he identify? It is not sufficient to say that he knows 'a few letters'. His tuition should take into account exactly what he knows. (This observation task should take 5 to 10 minutes.)

Administration

Test all letters, lower case and upper case. The large print alphabet on page 45 should be used. It could be copied or removed from the book and mounted on a clipboard for this purpose. Ensure that the child reads *across* the lines so that the letters are treated in a random order (and not in alphabetical order).

Use only the following questions to get the child to respond to the letters. *Do not ask only for sounds, or names.*

To introduce the task: *Start with*: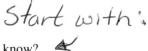
- What do you call these?
- Can you find some that you know? ✏

Pointing to each letter in horizontal lines:
- What is this one?

If a child does not respond:
Use one or more of these questions and try to avoid bias towards any one of them.
- Do you know its name?
- What sound does it make?
- Do you know a word that starts like that?

Then moving to other letters:
- What is this? And this?

If the child hesitates start with the first letter of his name, and then go to the first line. Point to every letter in turn working across the lines. Use a masking card if necessary.

Scoring the record

- Use the Letter Identification Score Sheet (see page 46). Mark A for an alphabetical response, S for sound, or W for word beginning similarly, and record what the child says when the response is incorrect.

- Score as correct
  - an alphabet name
  - a sound that is acceptable for that letter
  - a response which says '... *it begins like* ...' giving a word for which that letter is the initial letter.

The scores given below apply when any one of these three criteria is used to mark a response correct. Obtain subtotals for each kind of response, alphabetical, sound or word beginning similarly, and note down for the record as a whole

- the child's preferred mode of identifying letters
- the letters a child confuses, so that they can be kept apart in the teaching programme
- the unknown letters.

Interpretation of scores

Tables which follow each observation task in this chapter show scores as Stanine scores for two large samples of children. For comparison choose the research group that best represents the group of children you will be testing. Choose the first table if you are assessing five-year-olds, or if the average Stanine score of 5 seems to fit with average progress in your school. Choose the second table if you are assessing six-year-olds, or if your children tend to move more quickly in this test area. It is also useful for a school to build up its own table of Stanine scores (Lyman, 1963).

Where a score on the table is allocated across more than one Stanine value, choose the lowest value.

Stanines distribute scores according to the normal curve in nine groups from 1 (a low score) to 9 (a high score) (see Lyman, 1963). They are normalised standard scores. Stanines can be used for normative test purposes to compare pupils one with another, and an individual child can be compared with other children. But a more important reason for using Stanines is so that an individual child's progress can be compared across various tests which have different ranges of scores (i.e., when raw scores are not comparable). They allow one pupil's progress to be compared on several quite different types of observations.

Following such testing, teaching should aim to improve the child's ability to distinguish letters one from another on any basis that works (not necessarily by letter-sound relationships). Expand the child's range of known letters allowing any distinction that works for that child. As more and more letters are controlled he becomes ready for systematic associations like alphabetical names and sound equivalents. *When he knows more he is more able to be flexible and consider alternatives.*

As it is possible for young children to completely master the particular set of letters in a language one would expect a child to move gradually over time through the Stanine score range until he reached perfect scoring for the symbols of the alphabet. An individual child's Stanine score indicates his status relative to all children in the age group. It is most useful to contrast a particular child's scores at two points of time to reflect progress.

Letter Identification scores are very sensitive to instructional procedures. The teaching of letter-sound relationships will result in most responses being sounds rather than names, and the whole set of letters may be learned earlier than under a different method of instruction. The 1968 sample of New Zealand children of mixed ethnic groups was slower to learn Letter Identification responses than another sample tested in 1978.

Research Group	Letter Identification (Normalised scores – Stanine groups)								
320 urban children aged 5:0–7:0 in 1968	**Stanine group**	1	2	3	4	5	6	7	8	9
	Test score	— 0 —		1–7	8–25	26–47	48–52	53	—— 54 ——	
282 urban children aged 6:0–7:3 in 1978	**Stanine group**	1	2	3	4	5	6	7	8	9
	Test score	0–13	14–28	29–43	44–49	50–52	53	—— 54 ——		

Reliability: 100 urban children aged 6:0, 0.97, split-half (Clay, 1966).
Validity: Correlation with Word Reading for 100 children at 6:0, 0.85 (Clay, 1966).

A	F	K	P	W	Z
B	H	O	J	U	
C	Y	L	Q	M	
D	N	S	X	I	
E	G	R	V	T	
a	f	k	p	w	z
b	h	o	j	u	a
c	y	l	q	m	
d	n	s	x	i	
e	g	r	v	t	g

LETTER IDENTIFICATION SCORE SHEET

Date: _____

Name: _____ Age: _____ TEST SCORE: [ ] /54

Recorder: _____ Date of Birth: _____ STANINE GROUP: [ ]

	A	S	Word	I.R.		A	S	Word	I.R.
A					a				
F					f				
K					k				
P					p				
W					w				
Z					z				
B					b				
H					h				
O					o				
J					j				
U					u				
					a				
C					c				
Y					y				
L					l				
Q					q				
M					m				
D					d				
N					n				
S					s				
X					x				
I					i				
E					e				
G					g				
R					r				
V					v				
T					t				
					g				
			TOTALS						

Confusions:

Letters Unknown:

Comment:

Recording:

A — Alphabet response: tick (check)

S — Letter sound response: tick (check)

Word — Record the word the child gives

IR — Incorrect response: Record what the child says

TOTAL SCORE [ ]

CONCEPTS ABOUT PRINT

A check (5 to 10 minutes) should be made on what children have learned about the way we print languages. Some of the important concepts that can be tested easily are: the front of the book, that print (not the picture) tells the story, that there are letters, and clusters of letters called words, that there are first letters and last letters in words, that you can choose upper or lower case letters, that spaces are there for a reason, and that different punctuation marks have meanings (fullstop, question mark, talking marks).

Even though we may have tried to explain some of these things we cannot assume that our verbal explanations have taught the children to use their eyes to locate, recognise and use this information. Concepts about print are learned gradually as the child reads and writes over the first two years of formal schooling.

The booklets required for the Concepts About Print observations are entitled *Sand* (Clay, 1972) and *Stones* (Clay, 1979). They can be used with the new entrant to school or the 'non-reader' because the child is asked to help the examiner by pointing to certain features as the examiner reads the book. Five-year-old children have

some fun and little difficulty with the test items. The test reflects changes in reading skill during the first year of instruction but is of less significance in the subsequent years for children who make average progress. For problem readers confusions about these arbitrary conventions of our written language code tend to persist.

Concepts About Print has proved to be a sensitive indicator of one group of behaviours which support reading acquisition. As non-readers become readers changes occur in Concepts About Print scores. This set of observations is able to capture changes over time in the first years of school. Concepts About Print has been translated and used with Danish- and Spanish-speaking children. Unfortunately, the interest in Concepts About Print has resulted in it being lifted from its position as one of a battery of observation tasks in a wide-ranging survey designed to monitor changes in a complex set of reading behaviours and it has been expected to stand alone as some indicator of 'readiness' or reading progress. I do not like to see it reduced to a mere prediction device when it can be used as a valuable guide for teachers in their teaching during the early stages of reading acquisition. Important though this learning is it addresses only *one* of several areas of necessary learning.

Some important discussions of the Concepts About Print observation task will be found in Clay (1989; 1991) and Johns (1980).

Administration

The tasks present a standard situation within which the child can be observed. Try to retain a standard task but be flexible enough to communicate the task to the child.

Administer the items according to the instructions given. If the child fails item 10 then items 12, 13 and 14 are likely to be failed and can be omitted at the discretion of the examiner. If items 12, 13 and 14 are omitted you should still read the story on those pages to the child. Items 15 to 24 should be administered to all children.

Use the instructions for the administration and scoring of this test given on pages 48 and 49. Use the scoring sheet on page 52.

Before starting, thoroughly familiarise yourself with this test. Use the exact wording given below in each demonstration. (Read the instructions from the printed text for each administration.)

On another day
I looked for that hole
All I saw was
flat sand, soft sand,
wet sand and waves.
But oh , no hole !

18

from *Sand*

and kicked it very hard.
I swung back my foot

10

from *Stones*

Say to the child: '*I'm going to read you this story but I want you to help me.*'

COVER

Item 1 Test: For orientation of book. Pass the booklet to the child, holding the book vertically by outside edge, spine towards the child.

Say: '*Show me the front of this book.*'

Score: 1 point for the correct response.

PAGES 2/3

Item 2 Test: Concept that print, not picture, carries the message.

Say: '*I'll read this story. You help me. Show me where to start reading. Where do I begin to read?*'

Read the text to the child.

Score: 1 for print. 0 for picture.

PAGES 4/5

Item 3 Test: For directional rules.

Say: '*Show me where to start.*'

Score: 1 for top left.

Item 4 Say: '*Which way do I go?*'

Score: 1 for left to right.

Item 5 Say: '*Where do I go after that?*'

Score: 1 for return sweep to left.

(Score items 3-5 if all movements are demonstrated in one response.)

Item 6 Test: Word by word pointing.

Say: '*Point to it while I read it.*' (Read slowly, but fluently.)

Score: 1 for exact matching.

PAGE 6

Item 7 Test: Concept of first and last.

Read the text to the child.

Say: '*Show me the first part of the story.*' '*Show me the last part.*'

Score: 1 point if BOTH are correct in any sense, i.e. applied to the whole text OR to a line, OR to a word, OR to a letter.

PAGE 7

Item 8 Test: Inversion of picture.

Say: '*Show me the bottom of the picture*' (slowly and deliberately). (Do NOT mention upside-down.)

Score: 1 for verbal explanation, OR for pointing to top of page, OR for turning the book around and pointing appropriately.

PAGES 8/9

Item 9 Test: Response to inverted print.

Say: '*Where do I begin?*' '*Which way do I go?*' '*Where do I go after that?*'

Score: 1 for beginning with 'The' (**Sand**), or 'I' (**Stones**), and moving right to left across the lower and then the upper line. OR 1 for turning the book around and moving left to right in the conventional manner.

Read the text to the child.

PAGES 10/11

Item 10 Test: Line sequence.

Say: '*What's wrong with this?*' (Read immediately the bottom line first, then the top line. Do NOT point.)

Score: 1 for comment on line order.

PAGES 12/13

Item 11 Test: A left page is read before a right page.

Say: '*Where do I start reading?*'

Score: 1 point for left page indication.

Item 12 Test: Word sequence.

Say: '*What's wrong on this page?*' (Point to the page number 12, NOT the text.)

Read the text slowly as if it were correct.

Score: 1 point for comment on either error.

Item 13   Test: Letter order.

Say: *'What's wrong on this page?'* (Point to the page number 13 — NOT to the text.)

Read the text slowly as if it were correct.

Score: 1 point for any ONE re-ordering of letters that is noticed and explained.

PAGES 14/15

Item 14   Test: Re-ordering letters within a word.

Say: *'What's wrong with the writing on this page?'*

Read the text slowly as if it were correct.

Score: 1 point for ONE error noticed.

Item 15   Test: Meaning of a question mark.

Say: *'What's this for?'* (Point to or trace the question mark with a finger or pencil.)

Score: 1 point for explanation of function or name.

PAGES 16/17

Test: Punctuation.

Read the text.

Say: *'What's this for?'*

Item 16   Point to or trace with a pencil, the full stop (period).

Item 17   Point to or trace with a pencil, the comma.

Item 18   Point to or trace with a pencil, the quotation marks.

Item 19   Test: Capital and lower-case correspondence.

Say: *'Find a little letter like this.'*

Sand: Point to capital T and demonstrate by pointing to an upper case T and a lower case t if the child does not succeed.
Stones: As above for S and s.

Say: *'Find a little letter like this.'*

Sand: Point to capital M, H in turn.
Stones: Point to capital T, B in turn.

Score: ***Sand:***   1 point if BOTH Mm and Hh are located.
Stones: 1 point if BOTH Tt and Bb are located.

PAGES 18/19

Item 20   Test: Reversible words.

Read the text.

Say: *'Show me was.'*
'Show me no.'

Score: 1 point for BOTH correct.

PAGE 20

Have two pieces of light card (13 × 5 cm) that the child can hold and slide easily over the line of text to block out words and letters. To start, lay the cards on the page but leave all print exposed. Open the cards out between each question asked.

Item 21   Test: Letter concepts.

Say: *'This story says* (**Sand**) *"The waves splashed in the hole"* [or (**Stones**) *"The stone rolled down the hill"*].
I want you to push the cards across the story like this until all you can see is (deliberately with stress) *just one letter.'* (Demonstrate the movement of the cards but do not do the exercise.)

Say: *'Now show me two letters.'*

Score: 1 point if BOTH are correct.

Item 22   Test: Word concept.

Say: *'Show me just one word.'*
'Now show me two words.'

Score: 1 point if BOTH are correct.

Item 23   Test: First and last letter concepts.

Say: *'Show me the first letter of a word.'*
'Show me the last letter of a word.'

Score: 1 point if BOTH are correct.

Item 24   Test: Capital letter concepts.

Say: *'Show me a capital letter.'*

Score: 1 point if correct.

Scoring

Score items as instructed on pages 48 and 49. Use the table below to convert these scores to a Stanine score.

Interpretation of scores

As the concepts about print measured in this observation task are a limited set of information which can be learned in the first years of school, young children will test low early in their schooling, and their Stanine scores should increase as their reading improves.

However, the test's greatest value is diagnostic. Items should uncover concepts to be learned or confusions to be untangled. For teaching purposes examine the child's performance and teach the unknown concepts. The items are not in a strict difficulty sequence, but some indica-

tion of difficulty is given by the 'Age Expectations for Items' table below which gives the age at which average children passed each item. (However, such data will be very dependent on the teaching programme and method-emphasis used in any particular school.)

Most of these Concepts About Print items tell us something about what the child is attending to on the printed page. The items in which the order of the letters or words has been changed are particularly sensitive to shifts in children's visual attention to detail in print. It is not immediately obvious to teachers who use Concepts About Print that there is a steep gradient of difficulty in items 12 to 14. Children usually notice the changed word order (12) before a change in first and last letters (13) or a change in the middle letters (14) buried within the word.

Research Group	Concepts About Print (Normalised scores – Stanine groups)									
320 urban children aged 5:0–7:0 in 1968	Stanine group	1	2	3	4	5	6	7	8	9
	Test score	0	1–4	5–7	8–11	12–14	15–17	18–20	21–22	23–24
282 urban children aged 6:0–7:3 in 1978	Stanine group	1	2	3	4	5	6	7	8	9
	Test score	0–9	10–11	12–13	14–16	17–18	19	20–21	22	23–24

Reliability: *40 urban children aged 5:0 to 7:0 in 1968, 0.95, KR (Clay, 1970). 56 kindergarten children in Texas 1978. Test-retest reliability coefficients 0.73–0.89, and corrected split-half coefficients 0.84–0.88 (Day and Day, 1980).*

Validity: *Correlation with Word Reading for 100 children at 6:0, 0.79 (Clay, 1966).*

AGE EXPECTATIONS FOR ITEMS (Age at which 50 percent of average European children pass an item; Clay, 1970)																								
ITEM	1	2	3	4	5	6	7	8	9	10	11	12	13	14	15	16	17	18	19	20	21	22	23	24
Age 5:0		×																						
5:6	×		×	×	×	×	×	×	×	×	×										×			
6:0																			×	×		×		
6:6												×	×		×								×	×
7:0														×		×	×	×						

QUICK REFERENCE FOR SCORING STANDARDS

1	Front of book.
2	Print (not picture).
3	Points top left at 'I took . . .' (*Sand*); 'I walked . . .' (*Stones*).
4	Moves finger left to right on any line.
5	Moves finger from the right-hand end of a higher line to the left-hand end of the next lower line, or moves down the page.
6	Word by word matching.
7	Both concepts must be correct, but may be demonstrated on the whole text or on a line, word or letter.
8	Verbal explanation, or pointing to top of page, or turning the book around and pointing appropriately.
9	Score for beginning with 'The' (*Sand*) or 'I' (*Stones*) and moving right to left across the lower line and then the upper line, OR, turning the book around and moving left to right in the conventional movement pattern.
10	Any explanation which implies that line order is altered.
11	Says or shows that a left page precedes a right page.
12	Notices at least one change of word order.
13	Notices at least one change in letter order.
14	Notices at least one change in letter order.
15	Says 'Question mark', or 'A question', or 'Asks something'.
16	Says 'Full stop', 'Period', or 'It tells you when you've said enough' or 'It's the end'.
17	Says 'A little stop', or 'A rest', or 'A comma'.
18	Says 'That's someone talking', 'Talking', 'Speech marks', 'Print' (from computers).
19	Locates two capital and lower case pairs.
20	Points correctly to both *was* and *no*.
21	Locates one letter and two letters on request.
22	Locates one word and two words on request.
23	Locates both a first and a last letter.
24	Locates one capital letter.

CONCEPTS ABOUT PRINT SCORE SHEET

Date: _____

Name: _____   Age: _____   TEST SCORE: [____ /24]

Recorder: _____   Date of Birth: _____   STANINE GROUP: [____]

PAGE	SCORE	ITEM	COMMENT
Cover		1. Front of book	
2/3		2. Print contains message	
4/5		3. Where to start	
4/5		4. Which way to go	
4/5		5. Return sweep to left	
4/5		6. Word by word matching	
6		7. First and last concept	
7		8. Bottom of picture	
8/9		9. Begin 'The' (*Sand*) or 'I' (*Stones*) bottom line, top OR turn book	
10/11		10. Line order altered	
12/13		11. Left page before right	
12/13		12. One change in word order	
12/13		13. One change in letter order	
14/15		14. One change in letter order	
14/15		15. Meaning of ?	
16/17		16. Meaning of full stop	
16/17		17. Meaning of comma	
16/17		18. Meaning of quotation marks	
16/17		19. Locate M m H h (*Sand*) OR T t B b (*Stones*)	
18/19		20. Reversible words *was, no*	
20		21. One letter: two letters	
20		22. One word: two words	
20		23. First and last letter of word	
20		24. Capital letter	

WORD TESTS

Standardised word tests are based on the principle of sampling from the child's reading vocabulary. They cannot be reliable until the child has acquired sufficient vocabulary to make sampling a feasible measurement strategy.

For early identification a different approach is required. Word lists can be compiled from the high frequency words in the reading materials that are adopted. The principle here is a sampling from the high frequency words of that restricted corpus from which the child has had the opportunity to learn. The following test was devised for children who were using the New Zealand 'Ready to Read' series (1963), a series which has since been revised. (See below for discussion of how such a test might be constructed from reading vocabulary which the young learner has already been exposed to.)

'Ready to Read' Word Test

It should be noted that any test of first year instruction must be closely linked to that instruction. The *most frequently occurring words* in whatever basic reading texts are being used will probably provide a satisfactory source of test items.

It was found for Auckland children that a list of 15 words systematically sampled from the 45 most frequently occurring words in the 12 little books of the 'Ready to Read' series was a very good instrument for ranking or grouping children during the *first year* of instruction and for low progress readers in the second year (Clay, 1966). This test takes about two minutes to administer. The test sheet (page 55) can be copied and mounted on a clipboard for easy administration.

Administration

Ask a child to read *one* list. Give List A *or* List B *or* List C. Help the child with the practice word if necessary and never score it. Do not help with any other words and do not use the list for teaching. Use alternative lists for retesting.

Use of the test

The score will indicate the extent to which a child is accumulating a reading vocabulary of the most frequently used words in the 'Ready to Read' series during his first year at school.

The scores may be used, together with teachers' observations recorded for book reading, for grouping children. Successive tests will indicate whether a progressive change is occurring in the child's reading skill.

Scoring

The table on page 54 shows scores on the 'Ready to Read' Word Test as Stanine scores for a large sample of children aged five to seven years. (Stanines distribute scores according to the normal curve in groups from 1, the lowest, to 9.) It is possible for children to completely master this learning. One would therefore expect a child to move through the Stanine score range until he reached perfect scoring.

What the test does not do

- It does not give a reading age.
- It does not discriminate between better readers after one year of instruction. On the contrary it groups them together.
- Differences of less than three score points are not sufficiently reliable to support any decisions about the child's progress, without other evidence.
- It does not sample a child's reading skill if he is working beyond the level of early reading books.

Two other 'first' word tests

To support the use of this Observation Survey for one particular programme [Reading Recovery] in Australia and in the United States two other word tests have been constructed. The Ohio Test is republished in the Appendices to this book by permission of the authors, and the Canberra Word Test is listed in the References.

These two tests were constructed in different ways. The Canberra Word Test was developed for use with Australian children by Clough, McIntyre and Cowey (1990), following closely the model used to construct the 'Ready to Read' Word Test but using as a source the high frequency words in reading materials used in Canberra schools in 1989. The reading books published under the series titles 'Sunshine' and 'Storybox' form the bulk of the reading material from which the words were drawn. Teachers may find that the Canberra Word Test is suitable for use in other countries where 'Sunshine' and 'Storybox' books are used.

The Ohio Word Test was constructed in a different way, using the high frequency words from the Dolch Word List; the method of construction is described in Pinnell, Lyons, Young and Deford (1987). The administration procedures are the same as those used in the 'Ready to Read' Word Test (see Appendix 1, pages 86–87).

Research Group	'Ready to Read' Word Test *(Normalised scores – Stanine groups)*									
320 urban children aged 5:0–7:0 in 1968	Stanine group	1	2	3	4	5	6	7	8	9
	Test score	0	0	1	2–5	6–12	13–14	——— 15 ———		
282 urban children aged 6:0–7:3 in 1978	Stanine group	1	2	3	4	5	6	7	8	9
	Test score	0–1	2–5	6–9	10–12	13–14	——— 15 ———			

Reliability: 100 urban children aged 6:0, 0.90, KR (Clay, 1966).
Validity: Correlation was 0.90 for Word Test at 6:0 with Schonell R1 at 7:0 for 87 children.

Other reading tests

Once the child who entered school at five years has a reading level of 6:0 to 6:6 several standardised tests can be applied. A word test such as the Schonell R1, the Burt Word Reading Test (NZCER, 1981), the Canberra Reading Test, the Ohio Reading Test, or the British Abilities Scale Word Test cannot describe the child's integrated system of reading behaviours because this can only be observed on continuous text. Word tests will rank a child in relation to other children on reading vocabulary (knowledge of words in isolation).

The Schonell test was used in many New Zealand studies because research demonstrated clearly that the score for the Word Test of 15 words (described on page 53) could be added to the score for the first 30 words of the Schonell R1 test to give a combined score which was psychometrically a good measure of reading of New Zealand children between five and seven years (Clay, 1966). This has now been replaced in New Zealand by a local standardisation of the Burt Word Reading Test (1981) which describes children's level of attainment as a range rather than a reading age (allowing for the variations that occur in testing which create measurement error). In most countries there will be normative word tests commonly used in schools which can be added to

the test battery to provide two kinds of information:

1 A sample of the reader's competence with reading words in isolation, and
2 how this compares with the normative performance of the child's age group.

To assess children reading continuous text teachers could use a standardised oral reading test which uses paragraphs or short extracts, like the Neale Analysis of Reading Ability (ACER, 1988; NFER-Nelson, 1989), to make running record-type observations. This would allow for observations of the child's text-reading behaviour in a situation which is standard and which is graded in difficulty. A teacher who has thought about the reading process can extract much more information about the child's system of operating on cues in reading from a running record on a paragraph reading test than is yielded only by the test scores on this test.

For children whose reading level is above the average after two years of instruction, other graded paragraphs are available in standardised tests designed for groups. These texts can provide some evidence of the children's use of meaning, sentence structure cues, and orthographical and phonological information (for example, see Watson and Clay, 1975).

LIST A	LIST B	LIST C
Practice Word the	Practice Word said	Practice Word is
I	and	Father
Mother	to	come
are	will	for
here	look	a
me	he	you
shouted	up	at
am	like	school
with	in	went
car	where	get
children	Mr	we
help	going	they
not	big	ready
too	go	this
meet	let	boys
away	on	please

WORD TEST SCORE SHEET

Use any **one** list of words.

Date: _____

Name: _____

TEST SCORE: [   ] /15

Age: _____ Date of Birth: _____

STANINE GROUP: [   ]

Recorder: _____

Record incorrect responses beside word

LIST **A**	LIST **B**	LIST **C**
I	and	Father
Mother	to	come
are	will	for
here	look	a
me	he	you
shouted	up	at
am	like	school
with	in	went
car	where	get
children	Mr	we
help	going	they
not	big	ready
too	go	this
meet	let	boys
away	on	please

COMMENT:

WRITING

Examine examples of the child's writing behaviour. Does he have good letter formation? How many letter forms does he use? Does he have a small stock of words which he can construct from memory with the letters correctly sequenced? What are they?

By observing children as they write we can learn a great deal about what they understand about print, and messages in print, and what features of print they are attending to. Writing behaviour is a good indicator of a child's knowledge of letters and of the left-to-right sequencing behaviour required to read English. In writing words letter by letter the child must recall not only the configuration but also the details of letter formation and letter order. A child's written texts are a good source of information about his visual discrimination of print for as the child learns to write words, the hand and the eye support and supplement each other to organise the learner's first attempts to discover how to distinguish different letters one from another (a large set of visual discrimination learning).

Writing samples

Rating techniques can be used on children's early attempts to write stories. For example, to rate writing in the first year of school take three samples of the child's stories on consecutive days or for three successive weeks and rate them as follows for language level, message quality and directional features. (One sample is not sufficiently reliable for this evaluation technique.)

Language level
Record the number of the highest level of linguistic organisation used by the child.

1   Alphabetical (letters only).
2   Word (any recognisable word).
3   Word group (any two-word phrase).
4   Sentence (any simple sentence).
5   Punctuated story (of two or more sentences).
6   Paragraphed story (two themes).

Message quality
Record the number for the best description of the child's sample.

1   He has a concept of signs (uses letters, invents letters, uses punctuation).
2   He has a concept that a message is conveyed.
3   A message is copied.

4   Repetitive use of sentence patterns such as 'Here is a …'.
5   Attempts to record own ideas.
6   Successful composition.

Directional principles
Record the number of the highest rating for which there is no error in the sample of the child's writing.

1   No evidence of directional knowledge.
2   Part of the directional pattern is known: start top left, *or* move left to right, *or* return down left.
3   Reversal of the directional pattern (right to left and return down right).
4   Correct directional pattern.
5   Correct directional pattern and spaces between words.
6   Extensive text without any difficulties of arrangement and spacing of text.

RATING WRITING SAMPLES

	A LANGUAGE LEVEL	B MESSAGE QUALITY	C DIRECTIONAL PRINCIPLES
Not yet satisfactory	1 – 4	1 – 4	1 – 4
Probably satisfactory	5 – 6	5 – 6	5 – 6

Sometimes what children learn falls outside the limits of the analysis categories that teachers use. Michael was five and in his first year of school, but at home he had access to his father's computer. Unaided he 'pecked out' this story on the keyboard, by-passing the need to form letters.

> Mr. snowe by michael.
> wun cod and snowee morning a boy came out to plae and he made a snoe man and when it was nite time farethe cris mis came too visit adlaide.

The story combines local knowledge (of Adelaide, Australia) with story knowledge about 'snowee' mornings and snowmen which do not occur in Adelaide, and with fantasy knowledge about 'farethe cris mis'.

It is part of the fun of making careful observations of children who are writing that we can reflect on how they draw from diverse sources of knowledge as they construct their stories.

Writing vocabulary

I observed the writing of 100 children once every week in a research study. One thing I noticed was that the more competent children made lists of all the words they knew. These lists of words were very interesting.

Mark's list

Examine Mark's list, produced spontaneously at home when he was 5:11. Assuming that he was writing down the page, notice how a word he has just written seems to suggest another word he might write. Mark found words that started the same (It, is, in), that ended the same (at, bat, hat), that were opposites (come, go), that form a category of family names (Mum, Dad, Mark, Denise), that are the same but different (car, cat, bell, ball) and so on.

From observations like these one of my research students, Susan E. Robinson (1973) devised a useful observation task which has all the properties of a good test when it is used in the first two years of school. Robinson's writing vocabulary task is like a screen upon which the child can project what he knows — not only what we have taught him but what he has learned anywhere in his various worlds. The child samples his own universe of knowledge. This is appropriate because when learners are near the beginning of learning in a new field the kind of sampling of knowledge used in test construction does not work — what you are sampling for is in very short supply. At first there is not enough common knowledge among beginners to use such a sampling approach.

A task was constructed where the child was encouraged to write down all the words he knew how to write, starting with his own name and making a personal list of words he had managed to learn. This simple test was reliable (i.e., a child tended to score at a similar level when retested within two weeks) and had a high relationship with reading words in isolation. Even at kindergarten stage a child can respond to the instruction 'Write all the words you know.' How children respond changes over time, and highly competent children can demonstrate long lists of words even after a limited time at school.

This is an assessment that a teacher can do in any place at any time, needing nothing but her personal knowledge of how to make such observations and scoring them in systematic ways.

Although some children will write nothing or just the first letter of their name, other young children will write more than 40 words in ten minutes, the time allowed for this observation. This provides a score which correlates well with other literacy measures and changes over time, and has good measurement qualities. When the child can write more than 40 words the value of this score for telling us about change in literacy control diminishes. After that the teacher can begin to measure how the child works with a more traditional spelling or writing task.

So, like many observation tasks, this one is very useful for a short period of time (about two years), telling us how fast a child is building control over a basic writing vocabulary.

Once formal schooling begins, the distribution of scores on this observation task changes markedly with age. This is shown on the graph for children aged five-and-a-half when compared with two groups of six-year-olds (see page 60).

Writing Vocabulary scores are very sensitive to the instructional procedures of the classroom. High scores will be associated with very different programmes which (a) foster early writing or (b) place an emphasis on word learning. Low scores will be associated with programmes which (a) provide few opportunities for children to write or (b) encourage writing but expect only invented spellings.

In the first year of school there is probably a high degree of interdependence between reading words and writing words, but it should not be assumed that success in the first years of learning to read would be assured simply by teaching children to write words.

Administration

The child is allowed ten minutes to complete this task (an observation sheet is provided on page 61). Give the child a blank piece of paper and a pencil and then say:

> *I want to see how many words you can write.*
> *Can you write your name?*

(Start the 10 minute timing here.)

• If the child says 'No' ask him if he knows any single-letter or two-letter words. Say:

> *Do you know how to write 'is'* (pause), *'to'* (pause), *'I'?* and then suggest other words that he may know how to write (see below).

• If the child says 'Yes' say:

> *Write your name for me.*

When the child finishes say:

> *Good. Now think of all the words you know how to write and write them all down for me.*

Give the child up to 10 minutes to write the words he knows. When he stops writing, or when he needs prompting, suggest words that he might know how to write.

> *Do you know how to write 'I' or 'a'?*
> *Do you know how to write 'is' or 'to'?*

Go through a list of words that the child might have met in his reading books or might be able to work out how to write, for example: the child's name, I, a, is, in, am, to, come, like, see, the, my, we, and, at, here, on, up, look, go, this, it, me.

Continue for 10 minutes or until the child's writing vocabulary is exhausted. Prompt the child as much as you like with words he might be able to write. Be careful not to interfere with his thinking and his searching of his own repertoire. Very able children need little prompting

but sometimes it is necessary to suggest a category of words.
The following questions suggest some examples.

> *Do you know how to write any children's names?*
> *Do you know how to write things you do?*
> *Do you know how to write about things in your house?*
> *Do you know the names of things you ride on (or in)?*
> *Do you know how to write about things you eat?*
> *Do you know how to write . . . ?*
> *Do you know how to write . . . ?*

It is not a requirement of this observation that the child be able to read the words he has written.

Scoring

Correct spelling
Each completed word scores one point if it is correctly spelled,

• but not if the child accidentally writes a word that is correct but spontaneously tells you that it is another word. For example, he writes 'am' and says without prompting that it is 'on',
• and not when the observer realises from something else that the child does that he does not know what word he has written.

Reversed letters
The formation of individual letters (including the reversal of letters) does not influence the scoring except when the letter form represents a different letter. So, words with one or more reversed letters are correct when the intended letters are clear (e.g. 'buƨ' for 'bus') but are not correct if the reversed letter could be a different letter (e.g. 'bog' for 'dog').

Words written right to left
These are scored as correct only if the child actually wrote the letters from right to left. Individual letters may or may not be reversed which means that words scored as correct may have a mixture of reversed and correctly oriented letters.

Series of words
Each word is counted in a derived series like 'look, looks, looking,' or in a rhyming set or spelling pattern group like 'sat, fat, mat, hat'.

Capital letters
Capital letters are acceptable substitutions for lower case letters and vice versa.

Research Group	Writing vocabulary *(Normalised scores – Stanine groups)*									
282 urban children aged 6:0–7:03 in 1978	**Stanine group**	1	2	3	4	5	6	7	8	9
	Test score	0–13	14–19	20–28	29–35	36–45	46–55	56–70	71–80	81–

Reliability: 34 urban children aged 5:6 in 1972 (Robinson, 1973), 0.97, test-retest.
Validity: Correlation with reading; 50 urban children aged 5:6 in 1972 (Robinson, 1973), 0.82.

Stanine scores are provided above for only one group of children.

Interpreting the observation

Look at the graph from Robinson's study. Half of the children aged 5:6 could not write more than four to seven words. Only four children at this age wrote more than 13 words. The results for children aged 6:0 were far higher, the mean score for two samples being 27 and 30. Even with the 10 minute limit the writing vocabulary of able children was by no means exhausted. One child wrote 78 words in 10 minutes. There are marked individual differences among children in the first year of school.

A poor writing vocabulary may indicate that, despite all his efforts to read, a child is in fact taking very little notice of the visual differences in print. He requires an all-out teaching effort and a great deal of help to elicit early writing behaviours. In this learning the hand and eye support and supplement each other. Only later does the eye become the solo agent and learning becomes faster than in the eye-plus-hand learning stage (Clay, 1991).

Many kinds of experiences, in school and out of school, with letters, numbers, words, stories, drawing and life in the real world have enabled the child to learn many things about print such as where it is used and what kinds of things it can tell us. Despite a high degree of inter-dependence between reading and writing words, they are not necessarily linked, according to studies of spellers. Some children cannot read words that they can write, and vice versa. However, instructional programmes vary in the extent to which they allow or foster this reciprocity.

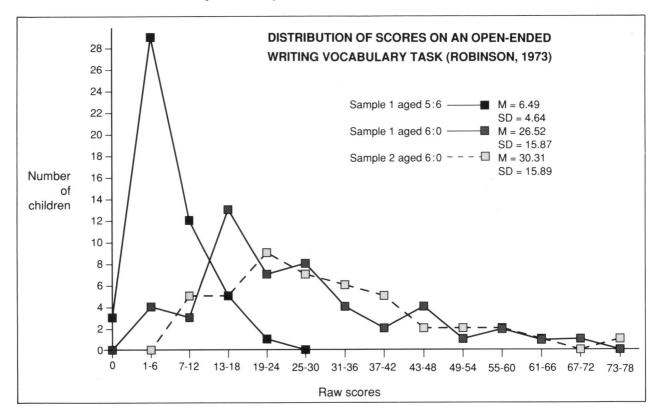

WRITING VOCABULARY OBSERVATION SHEET

Date: ───────────────

Name: ───────────────────── Age: ─────────────

Recorder: ─────────────────── Date of Birth: ───────────

(Fold heading under before child uses sheet)

TEST SCORE: [   ]

STANINE GROUP: [   ]

COMMENT

WRITING VOCABULARY WEEKLY RECORD SHEET

Name: _____

Date of Birth: _____

Initial Testing: Date:	Week: Date:	Week: Date:	Week: Date:	Week: Date:	Week: Date:
Week: Date:	Week: Date:		Week: Date:	Week: Date:	Week: Date:

Keeping records of progress

A record of a child's progress may be kept in one of the following ways.

An inventory of writing vocabulary
If the writing observation is done at several points of time — at entry, after six months and after one year, this provides one type of record of change over time in early writing. In the next example the progress of another child called Mark is clear from the record itself without any reference to scores or Stanines.

Recording change over time in daily or weekly writing
A teacher can keep a list of new words written independently by certain students to whom she is currently paying particular attention (see Writing Vocabulary Weekly Record Sheet, page 62).

Mark – writing vocabulary

A graph of writing progress

The teacher could make a graph of these accumulated totals. To start the record for Week 1 enter the number of words written correctly on the initial writing vocabulary observation task. Each week add, cumulatively, the number of new words the child wrote independently in the stories he was writing in the classroom. The cumulative record of writing vocabulary is a sensitive reflection of the child's increasing control over writing, and it is a reliable indicator of slow progress.

Running records of writing progress

It is surprisingly difficult to take running records of a young child writing with the teacher's assistance. In a classroom the teacher is either interacting with the child or allowing the child to interact with informed others to help the child as he writes. In several research studies students have tried to devise ways of recording what occurs in such observations but it turns out to be much more difficult than taking running records of reading. In a report which appeared in *The Reading Teacher* (May,

ACCUMULATED WRITING VOCABULARY

Name _____ Date of Birth _____

Numbers of words the child can write (y-axis: 0, 2, 4, 6, 8, 10, 12, 14, 16, 18, 20, 22, 24, 26, 28, 30, 32, 34, 36, 38, 40, 42, 44, 46, 48, 50, 52)

Date

Dates of observations

1991) there is a record which traces a child's progress in the first 10 weeks of school. That record had to be simplified leaving out many things that the observer saw. In that record it is possible to show the child becoming a more independent writer in a few weeks. It is also an interesting account of what the teacher was trying to achieve as she worked alongside the child. Those who wish to take observation records of children writing in authentic situations in interaction with teachers, children or other helpers should be warned to be ready for complicated sequences of behaviour.

Writing a story
An older child who can write 50 or more words is too competent for the use of the Writing Vocabulary task. He should be encouraged to write a story of several sentences or paragraphs (with as little help as possible) to provide a basis for grouping or categorising children's stories according to selected criteria. To assess change over time an earlier record for one child can be compared with a later one and the progress made should be clearly articulated.

Spelling
Older children can be given a spelling test which usually yields a normalised score. Spelling tests are often constructed with particular sets of words — regular words, irregular words, spelling 'demons', Greek roots, etc. Such constraints must be taken into account when interpreting the child's observed behaviour, and such behaviour should not be generalised to the writing of words outside the set of words used in the observation task.

Useful information from spelling observations is the evidence that is provided by watching the child at work and noting his strengths (words known, strategies that work, analogies that are tried). After the child has reached the upper threshold of his spelling achievement (where mostly correct spelling passes over to mostly incorrect spelling) the incorrect responses provide evidence of risk-taking, control of spelling patterns, the use of analogy, the rule-guided behaviour, and also of gaps, confusions or interfering or unproductive strategies. Sources used in New Zealand have been:

- Arvidson Spelling List (Arvidson, 1960)
- NZCER Basic Word List (Elley et al, 1977)
- The Spell-Write Word List (Croft, 1982)
- Peters' Spelling Test (Peters, 1970)
- Peters' Dictation Test (Peters, 1970)

HEARING AND RECORDING SOUNDS IN WORDS (DICTATION TASK)

This observation task was called dictation because the teacher asks the child to record a dictated sentence. But the child's product is scored by counting the child's representation of the sounds (phonemes) by letters (graphemes). Being able to hear the sounds in the words you want to write is an authentic task — a task one encounters in the real world rather than one devised merely for the purpose of testing. This observation task directs the attention of teachers and children to phonemic awareness, a current emphasis in the research literature.

School entrants can speak a language and need to learn to read and write it. They need to work out how every aspect of their spoken language relates to messages in print. Children need to learn how the language knowledge they already have can help them to read and write messages. One of the things they already know is how to use most of the sounds of their language. But how to work with the phonemes of a language is only one of the many things readers and writers need to know.

Recent research has made it clear that we must pay attention to four aspects of how the sounds of English are represented in print.

1   Children have to learn to hear the sounds buried within words and this is not an easy task.
2   Children have to learn to visually discriminate the symbols we use in print.
3   Children have to learn to link single symbols and clusters of symbols with the sounds they represent.
4   Children have to learn that there are many alternatives and exceptions in our system of putting sounds into print.

Children begin to work on relationships among a few things which they have learned long before they have learned all there is to know about letters and sounds. You do not have to know all the members of a set before you can work out some of the set's characteristics. Also, while some teachers are tediously teaching one letter-sound link after another in reading or writing, some children have already begun to read or write using bigger chunks of information.

- It is more efficient to work with larger chunks, and so they do!
- Sometimes it is more efficient to work with relationships rather than items of knowledge (like letters or words), and so they do!

- Often it is efficient to use a vague sense of a rule, and so they do!

They do not wait for the teacher to get through all her lessons on sounds before they begin working with larger chunks and relationships.

A useful observation task to capture the child's control of sound to letter links is 'Hearing sounds in words'. The teacher tells the child a sentence to be written. The child is encouraged to write what he can hear in the words dictated. What he does not hear will not get recorded. Scores show how successful the child was at hearing the sounds in the words and finding a possible way of recording those sounds in English spelling.

Administration

The observer ~~selects one of five alternative sentences to use in this observation task~~ (page 67). The child is given credit for every sound (phoneme) that he writes correctly, even though the whole word may not be correctly spelt. The scores give some indication of the child's ability to analyse the word he hears or says and to find a way of recording in letters the sounds that he can hear. Use an alternative form for retesting children.

Say to the child:

I am going to read you a story. When I have read it through once I will read it again very slowly so that you can write down the words in the story.

Read the test sentence to the child at normal speed. Then say:

Some of the words are hard. Say them slowly and think how you can write them. Start writing the words now.

Dictate slowly, word by word. When the child comes to a problem word say:

You say it slowly. How would you start to write it? What can you hear?

Then add:

What else can you hear?

If the child cannot complete the word say:

We'll leave that word. The next one is . . .

Point to where to write the next word if this helps the child.

Support the child with comments like these to keep the child working at the task.

When retesting use an alternative form to avoid practice effects. The alternative forms for this task are listed on page 67.

Recording

Use the form on page 70 for recording. Write the text below the child's version after the task is finished.

hm	skol	b
him	school	big

Scoring

The rules for scoring given here are necessary to ensure reliability and validity when the task is used for measurement of progress or change.

While initially the child's progress will be in the area of 'hearing and recording sounds in words', as he moves towards more control over writing we must expect him to be learning something about the orthography (the spelling rules and patterns) of the language.

Score one point for each sound (phoneme) the child has analysed and recorded that is numbered 1 to 37 on the examples (page 67), and record the total out of 37.

There can be no set of rules for scoring that will cover the ingenuity found in children's attempts. Scorers are advised to be conservative rather than liberal in applying the following scoring criteria if comparable results are to be achieved across different scorers.

The teacher who is a sensitive observer would note any partially correct responses which tell a great deal about the cutting edge of the child's knowledge. Such qualitative information is very important for planning the kind of help to offer the child.

[I am very aware of the arguments about developmental change from partially correct to correct responding. However, recorders do not agree on how to score partially correct responding and so for a reliable measuring instrument only the correct responding criteria for scoring can be recommended.]

Additions and omissions

If a letter does not have a number underneath it in the scoring standards on page 67 then it receives *no* score (even if a preceding letter has been omitted). Additions do not affect scoring as long as numbered letters are included.

tody	*Score 3*	todae	*Score 4*
today		today	

Alternative sentences

Select one of the following alternative Forms; A, B, C, D, or E.

Form A

```
I    h a v e    a    b i g    d o g    a t      h o m e
1    2 3 4       5    6 7 8    9 10 11  12 13    14 15 16
```
```
T o d a y   I   a m       g o i n g      t o   t a k e   h i m
17 18 19 20    21 22      23 24 25 26 27      28 29 30    31 32 33
```
```
t o    s c h oo l.
34 35  36 37
```

Form B

```
M u m    h a s    g o n e    u p   t o   t h e   s h o p.
1 2 3    4 5 6    7 8 9      10 11 12 13  14 15   16 17 18
```
```
S h e    w i l l    g e t    m i l k    a n d
19 20    21 22 23   24 25 26  27 28 29 30  31 32 33
```
```
b r e a d.
34 35 36   37
```

Form C

```
I    c a n    s e e    t h e    r e d
1    2 3 4    5 6      7 8       9 10 11
```
```
b o a t    t h a t    w e    a r e    g o i n g
12 13 14   15 16 17   18 19  20 21    22 23 24 25 26
```
```
t o    h a v e    a   r i d e    i n.
27 28  29 30 31   32  33 34 35   36 37
```

Form D

```
T h e    b u s    i s    c o m i n g.    I t
1 2      3 4 5    6 7    8 9 10 11 12 13  14 15
```
```
w i l l    s t o p    h e r e    t o   l e t    m e
16 17 18   19 20 21 22  23 24 25   26 27  28 29 30   31 32
```
```
g e t    o n.
33 34 35  36 37
```

Form E

```
T h e    b o y    i s    r i d i n g    h i s    b i k e.
1 2      3 4      5 6     7 8 9 10 11 12  13 14 15  16 17 18
```
```
H e    c a n    g o    v e r y    f a s t    o n    i t.
19 20  21 22 23  24 25  26 27 28 29  30 31 32 33  34 35  36 37
```

Capital letters
Capital letters are acceptable substitutions for lower case letters and vice versa.

Substitutions
Given what is being observed in this task it makes sense to accept a response when the sound analysis has been a useful one, even though the child has used graphemes which can record the sound but in this particular case the spelling is incorrect.

As a general principle substitute letters are acceptable if, in English, the sound is sometimes recorded in that way. Consonant substitutions which count as correct are:

$\dfrac{\text{skool}}{\text{school}}$	$\dfrac{\text{tace}}{\text{take}}$

and vowel substitutions which count as correct are:

$\dfrac{\text{cum}}{\text{come}}$	$\dfrac{\text{bak}}{\text{bake}}$

As children try to analyse the sounds in vowels they are likely to substitute unusual analyses of diphthongs:

$$\frac{\text{todae}}{\text{today}}$$

a substitution which does not alter the scoring.

Children may even replace one vowel with a letter that represents a vowel made in a neighbouring area of the mouth:

$$\frac{\text{vare}}{\text{very}}$$

It may seem arbitrary to some readers but given that the children are reading English I would score the e for y

substitution as acceptable and the a for e substitution as unacceptable, in the immediately preceding example.

Changes in letter order
Where the child has made a change in letter order take one mark off for that word. For example:

$$\frac{\text{ma}}{\text{am}} \quad 2-1=1 \qquad \frac{\text{gonig}}{\text{going}} \quad 5-1=4$$

Reversed letters
Reversed letters are not correct if they could represent a different letter. Another criterion that can be used is that if the letter used never makes the sound(s) being recorded, the substitutions used count as errors, as in:

$\dfrac{\text{dig}}{\text{big}}$	$\dfrac{\text{bog}}{\text{dog}}$

Making notes on other observations
It is important that the observer also make notes on the following:

- any sequencing errors
- the omission of sounds
- unusual use of space on the page
- unusual placement of letters within words
- partially correct attempts
- and 'good' confusions.

Any of these may tell the teacher something about what the learner knows and how the teacher may support some shift in performance.

Scoring standards
Use the scoring standard for the form you selected (A, B, C, D or E). See page 67.

Research Group	Hearing and Recording Sounds in Words (Dictation Task) *(Normalised scores – Stanine groups)*								
282 urban children aged 6:0 – 7:3 in 1978	Stanine group	1	2	3	4	5	6	7	8	9
	Test score	0–3	4–9	10–17	18–27	28–31	32–35		36–37	

Observing change over time

Timothy scored quite well on Hearing Sounds in Words. In February he recorded 19 phonemes out of 37. Five months later when he was retested he had a score of 30.

Susan Robinson and Barbara Watson devised and used the Hearing Sounds in Words observations during the development of the Reading Recovery programme. They proved to be valuable indicators of change over time of a child's ability to go from his analysis of sounds in spoken words to written forms for representing these sounds. In that sense this is not a true dictation or spelling test.

A teacher would normally use an alternative form when retesting a child. Here, Form A has been used for an early and a later testing to demonstrate to the reader how much the child's behaviour has changed.

Sentences: I have a big dog at home. Today I am going to take him to school.

Hearing and Recording Sounds in Words (Dictation Task), comparison of an early and later testing.

HEARING AND RECORDING SOUNDS IN WORDS (DICTATION TASK)
OBSERVATION SHEET

Date: _____

Name: _____ Age: _____

Recorder: _____ Date of Birth: _____

(Fold heading under before child uses sheet)

TEST SCORE: [   ] /37

STANINE GROUP: [   ]

COMMENT

6 SUMMARISING THE OBSERVATION SURVEY RESULTS

In the summary of the Observation Survey the teacher brings together what she has observed. She describes what the child can do, and what is partially known, at the boundaries of his knowledge as it were. Teachers should decide for which children they need a full analysis of the Observation Survey. They may, for example:

- make notes on teaching points for competent children
- make brief summaries for a broad average group
- produce detailed write-ups for children whose progress really puzzles them.

From the detailed information which the Survey yields, a first step towards an integrative summary is to summarise the results under the headings listed on two Observation Survey Summary Sheets as follows.

Book reading
Transfer the detail of the running records obtained at three levels and the analysis of cues used and cues neglected on to Sheet 1 (page 75).

Other observation tasks
Summarise the results of the other observation tasks and data on to Sheet 1 (page 75).

Analysis of strategies used by the child
On Sheet 2 (page 76) the teacher makes an analysis of the ways in which this child approaches and solves problems or new challenges. Complete each section under useful and problem strategies on text, with words and with letters. Use the questions on pages 72 and 73. Comments should be made on the child's performance in relation to each of the following six topics:

- Useful strategies on text.
- Problem strategies on text.
- Useful strategies with words.
- Problem strategies with words.
- Useful strategies with letters and sounds, separately and in clusters.
- Problem strategies with letters and sounds, separately and in clusters.

LOOKING FOR STRATEGIES

There are several reasons for this approach to summarising the Observation Survey.

- Any language is organised hierarchically on several levels. Only three have been selected here — text (a general term to stand for phrase, sentence or larger text), word level, and letter level.
- It has been argued (Clay, 1991) that although the reader appears to have stored many items of knowledge he has also learned strategies for working with the information in print — ways of finding it, storing it, filing it, retrieving it, and linking or cross-referencing one kind of information with another kind.

Good observation rather than modern linguistic theory led a talented reading clinician, Grace Fernald (1943), to formulate these statements about the relationships of letters, words and texts in reading.

'Groups of words must be the focus of attention in reading. Attending to the words as separate units, as in word-by-word reading, loses important meanings. The meaning of a word can vary with the group in which it occurs or, in another way, a group of words has a certain meaning. The sentence is the context in which the *meaning of the word group* is confirmed. The known word is the unit at which level the precision of the word group is usually confirmed.'

'For the unknown, unfamiliar, forgotten or misperceived word the reader's attention must go to clusters of letters or even to individual letters but whether these are right or not must be confirmed at the level of the word unit.'

She insisted therefore that in writing the word should always be written as a unit, and in reading words should always be used in context.

The questions listed in the next section helped some teachers to describe the reading strategies that young children use. Some examples of what is meant by reading strategies are given in Katy's records (page 74) and in the case reports of Mary and Paul (pages 77 and 78).

USEFUL STRATEGIES ON TEXT

Look at the Running Record of book reading where the child is performing adequately (90 to 100 percent accuracy) and try to find some evidence of how effectively he works with the sequences of cues. Also look at Concepts About Print items. Use these questions as a guide to your analysis of the records.

Location and movement
Does he control directional movement?
  – left to right?
  – top to bottom?
  – return sweep?
Does he locate particular cues in print? Which cues?
Does he read word by word? If so, is this a new achievement (+) or an old habit (–)?

Language
Does he control language well?
Does he read for meaning?
Does he control book language?
Does he have a good memory for text?
Does he read for the precise message?

Behaviour at difficulties
Does he seek help?
Does he try again?
Does he search for further cues? How?
Note unusual behaviours.

Error substitutions
Do the error substitutions the child uses make sense with the previous text? (Meaning)
Do they continue an acceptable sentence in English? (Structure)
Could they occur in grammar for that sentence, up to that word?

Is the child getting to new words from known words by analogy? For example, from *name* to *game* or from *play* and *jump* to *plump*.
Do some of the letters in the error match with letters in the text? (Use visual or graphic cues.)

Self-correction
Does he return to the beginning of the line?
Does he return back a few words?
Does he repeat the word only?
Does he read on to the end of the line (a difficult and confusing strategy for young readers)?
Does he repeat only the initial sound of a word?
Note unusual behaviour.

Cross-checking strategies
At an early stage of text reading
  – does he ignore discrepancies?
  – does he check language with movement?
  – does he check language with visual cues?
  – does he try to make language, movement and visual cues line up?

USEFUL STRATEGIES WITH WORDS

Check Concepts About Print (CAP), Text reading, Writing Vocabulary, Hearing Sounds in Words (Dictation) and Word tests.

The visual features of words
On CAP recognises line rearrangement.
On CAP recognises word rearrangement.
On CAP recognises that the first and last letters are rearranged.
On CAP recognises that the medial letters are rearranged.

On text can attend to detail.
Responds to initial letters.
Responds to initial and final letters.
Relates to some prior visual or writing experience of that word.

On Writing Vocabulary the child knows some words in every detail.

The sounds of words
Can hear the individual words in a sentence.
Can articulate words slowly.
Can break up words into sounds (as in a dictated sentence).

Attempts to write new words using a sound analysis.
Builds a consonant framework for a new word.
Knows that vowels are difficult and works at them.
Re-reads what he has written, carefully.

USEFUL STRATEGIES WITH LETTERS

Check Concepts About Print, Text reading, Letter Identification, Writing Vocabulary, Hearing Sounds in Words (Dictation) and Word tests.

Movement
Does the child form (write) some letters easily?
Does he form many letters without a copy?

Visual
Which letters can he identify?
How does he identify them?
Which letters does he use as cues in reading?
Could he detect an error because of a mismatch of
   letters?
(Which letters were difficult?)
(Which letters were confused one with another?)

Sounds
How does a child attempt a word in the Hearing Sounds
   in Words (Dictation) task?
Does he articulate it slowly?
Can he isolate the first sound of a word that he hears?
Can he give other words that start with the same sound?
Can he make/read/write other words that end with the
   same spelling pattern or inflection?

SUMMARISING THE SURVEY

The way of summarising the survey results adopted in the summary sheet is incomplete in that it does not tell the teacher how to search for those strategies which relate one level of linguistic organisation to another, letters to words, and words to their meaningful contexts. Research has not addressed many of these questions in ways which the observing teacher can use at this point in time. We do not yet know much about such in-the-head strategies.

Writing up the survey summary
Using only the evidence you have been reporting describe in a few lines the child's current way of responding. Point out what he can and cannot do on text reading and text writing. Indicate how his strategies (the ways in which he works) on word and letter levels help or hinder his getting messages from text. This statement is crucial for the teacher because it forces her to bring all the information on the reader who has been observed together in an overview statement. This could be the starting point of a programme of individual help.

The way in which Katy's teacher wrote about her strategies on texts, words and letters in the summary that followed the Observation Survey is shown on page 74. Katy's literacy achievement after one year in school was sufficiently low to warrant her referral to an early intervention programme.

WHAT DOES THIS SUMMARY MEAN FOR THE CHILD IN THE CLASSROOM?

The teacher will have gathered much information about the child during the administration of the observation tasks. (She will have more understanding of these many observations if she has pulled together their collective message in the Survey Summary.) What does the Observation Survey now imply for her classroom practice? It is useful to ask the following questions.

Books? What does the Survey imply about the way new books are introduced to this child? Is a rich introduction required? Or is the child able to approach a new book with minimal preparation or guidance? Are there indications that other types of text need to be part of this child's reading? Do the books you are using support this child, allowing him to use what he knows in the service of trying new texts?

Writing? Is there any aspect of writing that requires special attention? Does the child analyse the sounds in words and try to find ways of writing them? Does the child ask for feedback on his attempts? Does the child have a core vocabulary of high frequency words to support his story writing? What kinds of help does your classroom provide for the child to get to new words on his own?

Your programme? Do the results from several children tell you anything about (a) the emphases of your programme? and (b) the things you tend to be overlooking? Consistent patterns across children in reading and writing behaviours may provide evidence of emphases which you never intended or confusions you had never

Useful strategies on text:

Katy controls directional movement and one-to-one correspondence. She uses visual cues of initial letters, meaning cues sometimes and to a lesser extent structure cues. She does some rerunning and repeating to confirm and/or check. She is able to cross-check language with visual cues and self-corrects as a result.

Problem strategies on text:

She does not control book language well and at the hard level, structure and meaning tend to be overriden by visual cues. She does not rerun or seek help at difficulties. She does not read for the precise message. She uses minimal cross-checking of meaning, structure and visual cues, and minimal self-correction.

Useful strategies with words:

On text she is able to attend to detail especially initial letters. In Hearing Sounds In Words she can hear the individual words in a sentence and isolate and record some initial, final and dominant consonants in words. She has a small core of high frequency words which she can write.

Problem strategies with words:

On CAP she does not recognise line, word or letter rearrangement. On text she doesn't attend to letter detail consistently especially medial and final letters. In writing and hearing sounds she cannot always hear and record the correct consonant, and there is occasional sequencing difficulty.

Useful strategies with letters:

Katy identifies letters dominantly by alphabet response but occasionally gives a word or sound response. She can analyse some sound-to-letter relationships and some letter-to-sound relationships on text. She can write some letters with reasonable ease and form many letters without a copy.

Problem strategies with letters:

She does not always use her letter knowledge to identify the precise detail of a word. She confuses some letters in Letter Identification. On CAP she failed to locate both examples of upper/lower case correspondence, one and two letters and the capital letter.

SUMMARY

Katy is reading at Book Level 3. She has control over early strategies of directionality and one-to-one matching of words and seems to be able to locate some known and unknown words on text. She tends to use visual cues dominantly and sometimes uses meaning cues but does not always attend to structure cues to elicit the precise meaning of text. Limited repetition and rerunning and minimal self-correction appear to indicate she is not always monitoring and using strategies to cross-check for the precise detail of print. She can recognise and write some words and can analyse some letters from sound to letter but is not able to process and integrate this information effectively on text and in writing.

SIGNATURE:

How Katy's teacher summarised
Katy's Observation Survey.

OBSERVATION SURVEY SUMMARY SHEET

Recommended for survey checks after one year of instruction

Name: _____ Date: _____ D. of B. _____ Age: ____ yrs ____ mths

School: _____ Recorder: _____

Text Titles	**Running words** **Error**	**Error rate**	**Accuracy**	**Self-correction rate**
1. Easy _____	_____	1: _____	_____ %	1: _____
2. Instructional _____	_____	1: _____	_____ %	1: _____
3. Hard _____	_____	1: _____	_____ %	1: _____

Directional movement _____

Analysis of Errors and Self-corrections
Cues used or neglected [Meaning (M) Structure or Syntax (S) Visual (V)]

Easy _____

Instructional _____

_____

Hard _____

_____

Cross-checking on cues (Note that this behaviour changes over time)

_____

_____

LETTER IDENTIFICATION

	54

CONCEPTS ABOUT PRINT   *SAND*   *STONES*

	24

WORD TEST (CLAY)   LIST A _____   LIST B _____   LIST C _____

	15

OTHER READING TEST _____

WRITING SAMPLE	WRITING VOCABULARY	HEARING SOUNDS IN WORDS (DICTATION)	STORY	SPELLING
Language:		A		
Message:		B		
Direction:		C		
		D		
		E		
		37		

Useful strategies on text:

Problem strategies on text:

Useful strategies with words:

Problem strategies with words:

Useful strategies with letters:

Problem strategies with letters:

SUMMARY:

SIGNATURE: _____

thought of. Are there confusions to be got rid of? Are there new things which you need to draw children's attention to? Do you have to think about more helpful and supportive texts? Do you need to provide more individual help for children to get their composed stories down on paper?

Next strategies? What changes in strategies would you wish to see these children making over the next three months of instruction? Will you expect them to be more independent of you and how is this to be achieved? An observation summary sheet for recording multiple testings is shown on page 79.

TWO EXAMPLES OF SURVEY SUMMARIES

I Mary aged 6 : 0 — early reading stage

Initial testing: 4.5.77
Initial status: Early reading — one line texts.

1 **Book reading**
Mary read three Caption Books: *I am Big* (seen), *The Bear Family* (seen) and *I am Little* (unseen) with 94, 87, 75 percent accuracy and 0 : 3, 1 : 5, 0 : 8 self-correction rates.

2 **Observation task results**
Mary's score on Letter Identification was 34/54, on Concepts About Print 13/24, on the Word tests 3/15 and 0/30, on Writing Vocabulary 2 and on the Hearing Sounds in Words task 8/37.

3 **Useful strategies on text**
Mary uses fluent book language. She moves across the print from left to right with return sweep.

Problem strategies on text
Mary's fluent language response overrides visual and locating cues. Under the tester's monitoring she *can* locate word by word and *can* attend to the words she knows in print (*I, am, is, here*), but when she works independently her language response is too fluent to allow any integration of cues. Her self-correction rates are low. She does not attend to letter cues. Her miscues had zero graphic correspondence.

4 **Useful strategies with words**
Mary recognised *I, here, am* in isolation. She wrote the sentence:

I si a May (for *I am Mary*)

She analysed some initial sounds (for, have, big, home) on the Hearing Sounds in Words task.

Problem strategies with words
Mary does not attend to words while reading unless asked to 'Look carefully and read with your finger'. Locating in print and coordinating finger and speech in word-by-word reading is a difficult coordination for her to make.

5 **Useful strategies with letters**
Mary identified 34/54 letters by name.
She knows some sound-to-letter relationships.

Problem strategies with letters
Mary's long list of confused letters implies that she does not know how to search for ways of distinguishing similar letter shapes (i.e. how to visually discriminate between the pairs).

I	F	I	j	q	g	i	r	b	h	k	j	b	b	O
L	E	T	f	u	y	l	q	d	n	x	i	p	g	Q

Summary
Mary has made some progress with the use of visual cues but her fluent language overrides visual cues and prevents word-by-word reading. Discrepancies do not signal to her to recheck and self-correct.

II Paul aged 6 : 9 — first reading books

Initial testing: 9.8.77
Initial status: First Readers

1 **Book reading**
Paul read *Early in the Morning* (seen) with 98 percent accuracy and 0 : 1 self-corrections and *The Lazy Pig* with 79 percent accuracy and 1 : 3 self-corrections.

2 **Observation task results**
Paul's score on Letter Identification was 31/54, on Concepts About Print 19/24, on the Word tests 3/15 and 4/30, on Writing Vocabulary 7 and on the Hearing Sounds in Words task 11/37.

3   Useful strategies on text

Paul predicts meaningful language from picture clues with 1 : 1 matching, using some initial letter-to-sound knowledge. He self-corrects some mis-matches and known words.

Problem strategies on text

His miscues have semantic and syntactic accept-ability but not graphic acceptability. He is very distractable and often uses diversionary tactics to escape the reading task.

4   Useful strategies with words

He identified few words in isolation. He wrote seven words. He uses his meagre word knowledge in reading text. He analyses some sounds within words.

Problem strategies with words

The recall of words seems to be a difficult area for Paul. His good language overrides word knowledge in reading.

5   Useful strategies with letters

He identified 31 letter symbols by letter name. He analyses initial sounds and some sounds within words. He uses some initial letters-to-sound knowl-edge in reading.

Problem strategies with letters

He confused more letters on Letter Identification

$$\frac{n}{u} \quad \frac{u}{y} \quad \frac{x}{z} \quad \frac{z}{x} \quad \frac{E}{F}$$

than in writing $\frac{W}{M}$, and he

needs to learn how to control these confusions.

Summary

Paul has shown progress in component skills of reading but his age and habituated diversionary tactics, his difficulty in recalling sight words and his overriding lan-guage response in reading text have prevented any rapid reading progress.

OBSERVATION SUMMARY FOR MULTIPLE TESTINGS

Name: _____

Date of Birth: _____

School: _____

SUMMARY OF RUNNING RECORD

Text Titles	Running words Error	Error rate	Accuracy	Self-correction rate

Initial Test Date: _____

1. Easy _____ _____ 1: _____ _____ % 1: _____

2. Instructional _____ _____ 1: _____ _____ % 1: _____

3. Hard _____ _____ 1: _____ _____ % 1: _____

Retest Date: _____

1. Easy _____ _____ 1: _____ _____ % 1: _____

2. Instructional _____ _____ 1: _____ _____ % 1: _____

3. Hard _____ _____ 1: _____ _____ % 1: _____

Further Test Date: _____

1. Easy _____ _____ 1: _____ _____ % 1: _____

2. Instructional _____ _____ 1: _____ _____ % 1: _____

3. Hard _____ _____ 1: _____ _____ % 1: _____

TESTS	L.I.		C.A.P.		Word Test		Reading	Writing		Hearing Sounds in Words	
	54	Stanine	24	Stanine	15	Stanine	Test Score		Stanine	37	Stanine
Initial test Date:											
Retest Date:											
Further Test (1)											
Further Test (2)											

RECOMMENDATIONS: (for class teacher, or for review, or further teaching, or further assessment)

7 THE TEACHER AND THE OBSERVATIONS

An observant teacher must respond sensitively to the individual child's next step into new territory. How can she do this?

1   She must be familiar with what the child already knows.
2   She must be close at hand as he reads and writes.
3   She must know how to support his next leap forward.
4   She must allow children enough space to be independent learners.

Such knowledge allows the teacher to guide literacy learning in individual children. The teacher must monitor the progress of individual school entrants otherwise her programme could be holding back the fast movers or dragging along those who approach literacy slowly and cautiously.

A teaching programme can be organised so that the teacher

- can observe how children are working and learning
- can make and keep records
- can monitor the progress of the competent children at *spaced* intervals
- and can monitor and guide the teaching of the less competent children at *frequent* intervals.

THE UTILITY OF OBSERVING READING BEHAVIOUR

Running records of text reading can be used whenever oral reading is appropriate. Teachers can use them in many ways.

1   *Capturing behaviour for later consideration.* When teachers take a running record as the child reads his book they find they notice more about what the child is trying to do. They can also look back over this record, replay in their minds exactly what the children said and did, check on the validity of their assumptions, and think about the behaviour. The record captures the behaviour of the moment.

2   *Quantifying the record.* If a teacher knows how many words there are in the text which the child reads she can quickly turn this behaviour into an accuracy score, and relate this to a gradient of book difficulty: unaided he reads Book Level Seven with 95% accuracy but Book Level Eight with 87% accuracy.

3   *A cumulative record.* Change over time can be captured with such records taken from time to time, during the child's usual reading to the teacher.

4   *Placement.* From such records teachers can place children in groups or classes in a school. A child who is changing his school can be quickly checked to see at what level he will succeed in a new school.

5   *For critical decisions.* Critical decisions about giving the young child special assistance of some kind, or rapid promotion, or a referral to the school psychologist can be supported with a report on the child's reading behaviour on texts, from a running record. I advised my child psychologist students to ask for such records (partly because it puts a responsibility on teachers to be observant and partly because it saves the psychologist's time).

6   *To establish text difficulty.* I think of reading progress as being able to read increasingly difficult texts with accuracy and understanding. Running records are used by teachers to try out a child on a book to test the difficulty level of the text in relation to the child's competencies. Having such a behavioural record of exactly how a pupil reads a particular text gives teachers confidence to allow different children to move through different books at different speeds. They know they can still keep track of individual progress.

7   *Observing particular difficulties.* Running records provide opportunities for observing children's confusions and difficulties. The teacher records every correct response with a tick and records all error and

self-correction behaviour. This provides evidence of how the child works on words in text, what success he has, and what strengths he brings to the task. A teacher can quickly decide what might be the next most profitable learning point for that child and can test this out during teaching.

8   *For research purposes.* The records of well-trained teachers taken on a series of texts with a known gradient of difficulty can yield a ranking of students on book level by accuracy. These will correlate highly with test scores in the first two to three years of schooling.

INFORMATION FOR THE EDUCATION SYSTEM

There are several ways that an education system or a school system or a cluster of classes in a school can gain information on performance in that *system* by observing reading behaviours.

1   *Programme emphases.* If a supervising teacher takes records of text reading with a wide sample of children she will quickly discover if the teaching programme is out of balance. Word by word reading, spelling out words, not attending to meaning, ignoring the first letter cues or word endings — all these will stand out clearly in the records. And so will the good outcomes like getting it all together smoothly, working on words in ways which surprise the teacher, enjoying the stories and commenting on possible plot and character outcomes, relating what is being read to other experiences.

2   *New programme features.* If a programme is changed and new emphases are introduced, running records can be used to monitor the effects. Do the desired changes in children's processing of texts show up on the records? Do the records suggest any minor adjustments, now, without waiting for the summatal assessment at the end of the year?

3   *Training teachers.* A running record is an assessment which leads the teacher to ask herself questions about the child's needs. As she takes a record a teacher may discover new behaviours and begin to think about learning in new ways. For example, sometimes the reader goes back, repeating himself,

rerunning the correct message. Why does he do that? He was correct. Could it be that the child is surprised by what he read and has rerun to *monitor* his own behaviour to ensure that it is correct? Monitoring one's own language activities has a great deal of relevance for learning. It is important and needs to be encouraged.

Another contribution to teacher training occurs when teachers keep today's record as a baseline, and over several occasions observe the child again, capturing progress. It is informative to look back at the records of the changes that have occurred.

4   *Information for lay persons.* Two groups who make demands on teachers in New Zealand are parents and administrators. We have been surprised at how impressed both groups have been with two outcomes of running records taken over time. Teachers have used graphs of the reading progress (see page 35) of children through their reading books in their appeals for resources to school management committees and School Boards. Parents have also been reassured by such records and by sharing with the teacher the folios of work which show the child's progressions in writing. We have found that behavioural records, if thoughtfully planned, communicate clearly to lay persons interested in education. *Note that it is not the actual running records that have been shared with lay people.*

As well as Running Records other observation procedures reported in this early intervention survey are Concepts About Print, Writing Vocabulary, Hearing Sounds in Words (Dictation), and Letter Identification. These can show teachers which children do not understand some basic concepts about books and print, or who is trying to read with little knowledge of letters, or which children seem to know words but are not noticing letter sequences within them. The confusions of young readers belong to all beginners: it is just that the successful children sort themselves out and the unsuccessful do not.

To minimise carelessness, bias and variability in observation records:

- there has to be a gradient of difficulty in the texts used for reading
- the teachers must be well trained. Six teachers scoring the same record should all get the same results. One teacher reading another teacher's record should be able to replay what the child actually said.

INFORMATION TO SUPPORT AN EARLY INTERVENTION FOR SOME CHILDREN

Early identification of children at risk in literacy learning has proved to be possible and should be systematically carried out not later than one year after the child has entered a formal programme. This gives the shy and slow children time to settle in and adjust to the demands of a teacher. It also overcomes the problems of trying to identify those who fail to learn to read before some of them have had a chance to learn what reading is about. In many ways it is sensible to try to predict this only after all children have had some equivalent opportunities to respond to good teaching.

Each child will differ in what is confusing, what gaps there are in knowledge, in ways of operating on print. The failing child might respond to an intervention programme especially tailored to his needs in one-to-one instruction. Teachers who had found the observation procedures useful for identifying the children who were in need of individual help asked me for further guidance. How should they teach those failing children? They were asking for specific teaching procedures which they felt they were not able to invent.

Most of the assumptions about reading achievement and reading difficulty would not lead us to expect that children who have difficulty would ever catch up to their classmates, or make continued *normal* progress. They would have to learn at greatly accelerated rates of progress to do that. The Reading Recovery development programme questioned whether such assumptions were well founded. We asked how many children given a quality intervention *early* in their schooling could achieve and maintain normal levels of progress? In other words, for what percentage of the children having reading difficulties was it really a question of never having got started with appropriate learning patterns?

A quality model of Reading Recovery (see Clay, 1993) provides several dimensions of assistance for a child in addition to his class programme.

- Firstly, a shift to one-to-one instruction allows the teacher to design a programme that begins where the child is, and not where the curriculum is. Any grouping of children for teaching forces a compromise on this position.
- Then, daily instruction increases the power of the intervention.
- The teacher strives to make the child independent of her (to overcome one of the major problems of reme-

dial tuition) and she never does for the child anything that she can teach him to do for himself.
- Acceleration is achieved by all the above means and also because the teacher never wastes valuable learning time on teaching something the child does not need to learn. She moves him to a harder text as soon as this is feasible but backs such progressions with quantities of easy reading.
- From sound theory of the reading process the child is taught 'how to . . .' — how to carry out operations to solve problems in text, how to monitor his reading, how to check his options, how to work independently on print.

It is not enough to have systematic observation procedures which monitor the progress of individual children. To be really effective a powerful second chance programme must be provided. It must be viable within the education system and it must have its own checks and balances to give quality assurance and quality control. It must 'live' in and adapt to small and large schools, small and large education systems, and different populations and reading programmes.

Many interventions for children with special needs never get to consider these issues. It is necessary to demonstrate:

- that the programme can work with children
- that teachers can be trained to make it work
- that the programme can fit into the organisation of the schools
- that it can be run and maintained within an education system.

In considering those issues I have learned that quality control of an intervention to recover failing children requires teachers who can make sensitive observations in systematic ways, but this is not sufficient. It also requires

- that teachers be trained concurrently in the conceptual and practical aspects of the programme
- that they understand the teaching procedures
- that they apply them consistently and critically
- that they can articulate and discuss their assumptions
- that they are supervised for a probationary period
- that those training teachers thoroughly understand the theory on which the programme and procedures were based
- that the teacher is a member of a school team which is mounting the intervention to reduce reading difficulties in that school
- that the education system supply resources for early intervention to save a higher outlay later to provide for older children still struggling with literacy.

AN OVERVIEW

Low achievers cannot profit from group instruction as easily as well-prepared children in the early years of school so we need to fine-tune our instruction towards their individual learning histories rather than buy another new curriculum or switch to a new method.

Systematic observation allows teachers to go to where the child is and begin teaching from there. Usually teachers say 'When you get to where our programme starts you will be "ready" for instruction; until then you are not ready.' It makes more sense for the teacher to become a sensitive observer of children during activities so as to help them make the transitions that have been planned for them.

A year at school will give most children a chance to settle, and to begin to try their abilities in literacy. Systematic observation will uncover which children are forming good or poor strategies, habits, skills, whatever you want to conceptualise as central to learning at this stage. It makes good psychological and administrative sense to find out before too long which children are becoming confused by standard educational practices, so that they can be offered alternative approaches to the same goals.

The teacher must monitor the changes that are occurring in the individual learner if she is going to fine-tune her programme. Otherwise she will be holding back the fast movers or dragging along the slow movers, already out of their depth. Low achievers can learn quite well if the teacher uses individual assessments to guide her teaching interactions with a particular child. The teacher needs assessments that tell her about the child's existing repertoire and how he is getting to those responses, and whether he is relating information from one area of competency to another. In literacy learning we are looking at ways of capturing:

- process
- repertoire
- strategies
- problem-solving (see Clay, 1991).

We want to record change over time in all these things as the child moves up a gradient of difficulty with increasing independence of teacher support.

If instruction is flexible enough to respect individuality in the first stages of new learning it can bring children gradually to the point where group instruction can proceed effectively with few confusions.

Observational instruments can arise from theory and can lead to research. A variety of theories may lead to observational tasks: measurement theory, or the psychology of learning, or developmental theory about change over time, or the study of individual differences, or theories of social factors and the influences of contexts on learning. Observational tasks direct teacher attention to the ways in which children are finding sources of information in texts and working with that information.

Typically this approach calls for time with individuals. There is an enormous mental barrier which says 'this is not a teacher's role.' I say, emphatically, it is! If the teacher can be more effective because she seeks and uses observational data to inform her teaching then we need tasks which fit easily into the busy schedule of a teacher's day. If possible we must find *good observational appraisals* which have *sound measurement characteristics* and which *can be used by the teacher on the run in day to day classroom practice*. Such assessments can be compared from one time to the next, from one classroom to the next, and from one school to the next.

APPENDICES

LIST A	LIST B	LIST C
PRACTICE WORD	PRACTICE WORD	PRACTICE WORD
can	in	see
and	ran	big
the	it	to
pretty	said	ride
has	her	him
down	find	for
where	we	you
after	they	this
let	live	may
here	away	in
am	are	at
there	no	with
over	put	some
little	look	make
did	do	eat
what	who	an
them	then	walk
one	play	red
like	again	now
could	give	from
yes	saw	have

For discussion of the Ohio Word Test, see page 53.

APPENDIX 1

OHIO WORD TEST SCORE SHEET

TEST SCORE

/20

Date: ————————————————————

Name: ———————————————— School: ————————————

Recorder: ————————————— Classroom Teacher: —————————

Record incorrect responses.
Choose appropriate list of words.   ✓ (Checkmark) Correct Response   ● (Dot) No Response

	LIST A	LIST B	LIST C
Practice words	can	in	see
	and	ran	big
	the	it	to
	pretty	said	ride
	has	her	him
	down	find	for
	where	we	you
	after	they	this
	let	live	may
	here	away	in
	am	are	at
	there	no	with
	over	put	some
	little	look	make
	did	do	eat
	what	who	an
	them	then	walk
	one	play	red
	like	again	now
	could	give	from
	yes	saw	have

APPENDIX 2   # Ohio Stanine Score Summary Sheet

Word Test

73 Ohio urban children first grade in 1990–91	Stanine group	1	2	3	4	5	6	7	8	9
	Test score	0–3	4–5	6–8	9	10–11	12–13	14–15	16–18	19–20

Reliability: 107 urban children, Autumn 1990, Cronbach Alpha = 0.92

Letter Identification

73 Ohio urban children first grade in 1990–91	Stanine group	1	2	3	4	5	6	7	8	9
	Test score	0–46	47–49	50	51	52	—— 53 ——		—— 54 ——	

Reliability: 107 urban children, Autumn 1990, Cronbach Alpha = 0.95

Concepts About Print

73 Ohio urban children first grade in 1990–91	Stanine group	1	2	3	4	5	6	7	8	9
	Test score	0–10	11–12	13	14–15	16	17–18	19	20	21

Reliability: 106 urban children, Autumn 1990, Cronbach Alpha = 0.78

Writing Vocabulary

114 Ohio urban children first grade in 1990–91	Stanine group	1	2	3	4	5	6	7	8	9
	Test score	0–7	8–12	13–16	17–19	20–24	25–30	31–36	37–40	41+

Reliability: Test-Retest (Spring 1990/Autumn 1990) N = 141: Pearson = 0.62

Hearing and Recording Sounds in Words (Dictation Task)

73 Ohio urban children first grade in 1990–91	Stanine group	1	2	3	4	5	6	7	8	9
	Test score	0–13	14–19	20–23	24–26	27–30	31–32	33–34	35	36–37

Reliability: 107 urban children, Autumn 1990, Cronbach Alpha = 0.96

Text Reading Level*

114 Ohio urban children first grade in 1990–91	Stanine group	1	2	3	4	5	6	7	8	9
	Test score	0–1	2	3	4–5	6–7	8–11	12–14	15–18	19–32

Reliability: 96 urban children, Autumn 1990, Rasch program for rating scale analysis (Wright, 1989): Person r = 0.83; Item r = 0.98.

* Scott Foresman Special Practice books (1979): Text Reading Level Administration materials, Copyright, 1989, The Ohio State University.

Note: Subjects (N = 155) were part of a two year study of kindergarten and first grade children in the Early Literacy Project (Pinnell, McCarrier & Button, 1989 – 91). Numbers may vary by subtest due to absenteeism or movement from the system. For each subtest the Autumn and Spring scores were averaged to determine a mid-year scoring range.

APPENDIX 2

New Zealand Stanine Score Summary Sheet

'Ready to Read' Word Test

320 urban children aged 5:0–7:0 in 1968	Stanine group	1	2	3	4	5	6	7	8	9
	Test score	— 0 —		1	2–5	6–12	13–14	— 15 —		

282 urban children aged 6:0–7:3 in 1978	Stanine group	1	2	3	4	5	6	7	8	9
	Test score	0–1	2–5	6–9	10–12	13–14	— 15 —			

Letter Identification

320 urban children aged 5:0–7:0 in 1968	Stanine group	1	2	3	4	5	6	7	8	9
	Test score	— 0 —		2–7	8–25	26–47	48–52	53	— 54 —	

282 urban children aged 6:0–7:3 in 1978	Stanine group	1	2	3	4	5	6	7	8	9
	Test score	0–13	14–28	29–43	44–49	50–52	53	— 54 —		

Concepts About Print

320 urban children aged 5:0–7:0 in 1968	Stanine group	1	2	3	4	5	6	7	8	9
	Test score	0	1–4	5–7	8–11	12–14	15–17	18–20	21–22	23–24

282 urban children aged 6:0–7:3 in 1978	Stanine group	1	2	3	4	5	6	7	8	9
	Test score	0–9	10–11	12–13	14–16	17–18	19	20–21	22	23–24

Writing Vocabulary

282 urban children aged 6:0–7:3 in 1978	Stanine group	1	2	3	4	5	6	7	8	9
	Test score	0–13	14–19	20–28	29–35	36–45	46–55	56–70	71–80	81–

Hearing and Recording Sounds in Words (Dictation Task)

282 urban children aged 6:0–7:3 in 1978	Stanine group	1	2	3	4	5	6	7	8	9
	Test score	0–3	4–9	10–17	18–27	28–31	32–35	— 36–37 —		

Where a score on the table is allocated across more
than one Stanine value, choose the lowest value.

REFERENCES AND FURTHER READING

Aman, M.G. and Singh, N.M. Specific reading disorders: Concepts of etiology reconsidered. In K.D. Gadow and I. Bader (Eds) *Advances in Learning and Behavioural Disabilities*, Vol. 2, pp 1–47, JAI Press, Greenwich, Connecticut, 1983.

Arvidson, G. *Alphabetical Spelling List*, NZCER, Wellington, 1960.

Brown, R. *A First Language. The Early Stages*, Harvard University Press, Cambridge, 1973.

Cazden, C.B. *Classroom Discourse: The Language of Teaching*, Heinemann Educational Books, Portsmouth, New Hampshire, 1988.

Clay, Marie M. 'Emergent Reading Behaviour'. Unpubl. doctoral dissertation, University of Auckland Library, 1966.

Clay, Marie M. 'The reading behaviour of five year old children: A research report'. *New Zealand Journal of Educational Studies* 2(1): pp 11–31, 1967.

Clay, Marie M. 'Reading errors and self-correction behaviour'. *British Journal of Educational Psychology* 39: pp 47–56, 1969.

Clay, Marie M. 'Research on language and reading in Pakeha and Polynesian children'. In D.K. Bracken and E. Malmquist (Eds) *Improving Reading Ability Around The World*, International Reading Association, Newark, Delaware, 1970.

Clay, Marie M. *Sand – the Concepts About Print Test*, Heinemann Publishers, Auckland, 1972.

Clay, Marie M. *What Did I Write?* Heinemann Educational Books, Auckland, 1975.

Clay, Marie M. *Reading: The Patterning of Complex Behaviour*, 2nd ed., Heinemann Educational Books, Auckland, 1979.

Clay, Marie M. *Stones – the Concepts About Print Test*, Heinemann Publishers, Auckland, 1979.

Clay, Marie M. *Observing Young Readers: Selected Papers*, Heinemann Educational Books, Portsmouth, New Hampshire, 1982.

Clay, Marie M. 'Concepts about print: In English and other languages'. *The Reading Teacher* 42(4): pp 268–277, 1989.

Clay, Marie M. *Becoming Literate: The Construction of Inner Control*, Heinemann, Auckland, 1991.

Clay, Marie M. *Reading Recovery: A Guidebook for Teachers in Training*, Heinemann, Auckland, 1993.

Clay, M.M., Gill, M., Glynn, T., McNaughton, T. and Salmon, K. *Record of Oral Language and Biks and Gutches*, Heinemann, Auckland, 1983.

Clay, M.M. and Imlach, R.H. 'Juncture, pitch and stress as reading behaviour variables.' *Journal of Verbal Behaviour and Verbal Learning*,10: pp 133–139,1971.

Clough, M., McIntyre, J. and Cowey, W. *The Canberra Word Test*, Schools and Community Centre, University of Canberra, 1990.

Croft, C. *Spell-Write: An Aid to Writing, Spelling and Word Study*, NZCER, Wellington, 1982.

Day, H.D. and Day, K. 'The reliability and validity of the Concepts About Print and Record of Oral Language'. Resources in Education, ED 179 932, Arlington, Virginia: ERIC Document Reproduction Service, 1980.

Department of Education. *Reading in the Junior Classes*, Learning Media, Wellington, 1985.

Elley, W., Croft, C. and Cowie, C. *A New Zealand Basic Word List*, NZCER, Wellington, 1977.

Fernald, Grace M. *Remedial Techniques in Basic School Subjects*, McGraw-Hill, New York, 1943.

Ferreiro, E. and Teberosky, A. *Literacy Before Schooling*, Heinemann Educational Books, Portsmouth, New Hampshire, 1982.

Genishi, C. 'Observational research methods for early childhood education'. In B. Spodek *Handbook of Research in Early Childhood Education*, The Free Press, New York, 1982.

Goodman, Y.M. and Burke, C. *The Reading Miscue Inventory*, Macmillan, New York, 1972.

Johns, J.L. 'First graders' concepts about print'. *Reading Research Quarterly* 15(4): pp 529–549, 1980.

Johnston, Peter H. *Constructive Evaluation of Literate Activity*, Longman, New York, 1992.

Lyman, H.B. *Test Scores and What They Mean*, Prentice-Hall, Englewood Cliffs, New Jersey, 1963.

McKenzie, M. *Journeys Into Literacy*, Schofield and Sims, Huddersfield, 1989.

Morrow, L.M. *Literacy Development in the Early Years*: *Helping Children Read and Write*, Prentice-Hall, Englewood Cliffs, New Jersey, 1989.

Neale, Marie D. *The Neale Analysis of Reading Ability*, Macmillan, London, 1958.
ACER, 1988.
NFER-Nelson, 1989.

New Zealand Council for Educational Research. *Burt Word Reading Test*, NZCER, Wellington, 1981.

New Zealand Council for Educational Research. *The Spell-Write Word List*, NZCER, Wellington, 1982.

Paley, V. *Wally's Stories*, Harvard University Press, Cambridge, Mass., 1981.

Peters, M.L. *Success in Spelling*, Cambridge Institute of Education, Cambridge, 1970.

Pinnell, G.S., Lyons, C.A., Young, P. and Deford, D.E. 'The Reading Recovery Program in Ohio', Volume VI (Technical Report). The Ohio State University, Columbus, Ohio, 1987.

Robinson, Susan M. 'Predicting Early Reading Progress'. Unpubl. MA thesis, University of Auckland Library, 1973.

Smith, F. *Understanding Reading*, 2nd ed., Holt Rhinehart and Winston, New York, 1978.

Stallman, A.C. and Pearson, P.D. Formal measures of early literacy. In L. M. Morrow and J. K. Smith (Eds) *Assessment for Instruction in Early Literacy*, Prentice-Hall, Englewood Cliffs, N.J. 1990.

Watson, S. and Clay, M.M. 'Oral reading strategies of third form students'. *New Zealand Journal of Educational Studies* 10 (1): pp 43–50, 1975.

Wells, G. *The Meaning Makers: Children Learning Language and Using Language to Learn*, Heinemann Educational Books, Portsmouth, New Hampshire, 1986.

INDEX